I0176558

"Wisdom That Transforms. Action That Lasts."

The Get Wisdom Commitment

At Get Wisdom Publishing we believe that true wisdom has the power to transform lives. Our mission is to equip readers with timeless insights and practical tools that inspire growth, guide decisions, and empower purposeful living. We don't just inform—we empower.

Our books combine profound understanding with real-life application, enabling readers to unlock their potential and navigate life's challenges with clarity and confidence. With each step guided by wisdom, we help you create lasting change and live the life you deserve.

When wisdom meets purpose, transformation follows.

The *OBSCURE* Bible Study Series

Grow in your faith through investigating unusual and obscure biblical characters.

"Deep Biblical Wisdom. Real-Life Faith Application."

The OBSCURE Bible Study Journey

The
Chosen Person

Keep Your Eyes on Jesus.

Personal Study Guide
Book 9

Faith isn't just about belief – it's about action.

Stephen H Berkey

GET**WISDOM**
PUBLISHING

COPYRIGHT

ISBN	978-1-952359-22-4	(Leader Guide, paperback)
ISBN	978-1-952359-23-1	(Leader Guide, ebook)
ISBN	978-1-952359-24-8	(Personal Study Guide, paperback)
ISBN	978-1-952359-25-5	(Personal Study Guide, ebook)
Audiobook available		(amazon.com and audible.com)

Bible Translations Used:

Unmarked scriptures and scriptures marked ESV are taken from THE HOLY BIBLE, ENGLISH STANDARD VERSION (ESV): Scriptures taken from THE HOLY BIBLE, ENGLISH STANDARD VERSION ® Copyright© 2001 by Crossway, a publishing ministry of Good News Publishers. Used by permission.

Scriptures marked NIV are taken from the NEW INTERNATIONAL VERSION (NIV): Scripture taken from THE HOLY BIBLE, NEW INTERNATIONAL VERSION ®. Copyright© 1973, 1978, 1984, 2011 by Biblica, Inc.™. Used by permission of Zondervan

Discover the biblical characters that mainstream studies forget – and the timeless lessons they teach."

TABLE OF CONTENTS

CONTENTS

FREE PDF RESOURCES

Living Wisely
The Life Planning Guide

A Quick-Start Guide to Purposeful Living and Wise Decisions!

Discover the five life domains: purpose, people, principles, productivity, and perspective. Wisdom is the ability to apply truth and logic to real-life decisions and produce good outcomes. It influences your choices and will produce action that lasts. Consider and apply the five practical wisdom principles for daily living.
(6 pages)

Free PDF: https://getwisdompublishing.com/resource-registration/

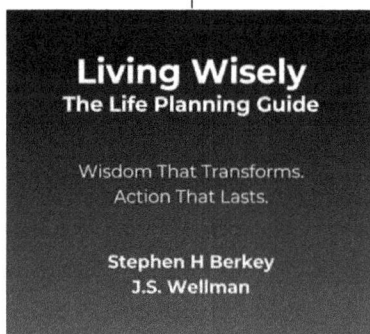

Living Wisely
The Life Planning Guide

Wisdom That Transforms.
Action That Lasts.

Stephen H Berkey
J.S. Wellman

Free PDF

Five Practical Principles For Life

When wisdom meets purpose, transformation follows.

Free PDF
Wise Decision-Making

[Get the ebook version for 99 cents]

You can make good choices.

This free resource provides a project-oriented perspective and gives ten detailed steps to analyze issues/problems to determine a solution. (26 pages)

Good decisions expand your horizons. Don't allow the fear of decision-making paralyze your ability to make good choices. Think through the reasonable alternatives and move forward. When your eyes are on the goal, making good decisions is easier.

Free PDF: https://getwisdompublishing.com/resource-registration/

Kindle ebook for 99 cents: https://www.amazon.com/dp/B09SYGWRVL/

Ebook

Free PDF

Make Thoughtful Decisions!

Good decisions expand your horizons.

Why Study OBSCURE Characters?

Unique, New, and Fresh

For experienced Bible students these characters will provide a fresh and interesting approach to Bible study. Since most of the material will be unfamiliar to the participants, new believers or those just starting Bible study should not feel intimidated by students who have been studying for years. Most readers will not be acquainted with the majority of the characters and events in this series.

Knowledge of Scripture

These studies are a great introduction for those just beginning Bible study. Regardless of their level of knowledge, everyone should find the characters and stories provide an opportunity to grow in their faith through investigating fascinating and unusual biblical stories and incidents.

Valuable Life Lessons

These lesser-known characters are a lot like you and me. God uses all sorts of people to accomplish His plans! You will become familiar with ordinary people, strange characters, and people living on the fringe of life who have the same troubles and challenges as people today. The deep truths and life lessons embedded in these studies should be valuable. They will provide new insights to scripture.

"Unlock Biblical Wisdom.
Transform Your faith!"

ABOUT THE LEADER GUIDE

All of the books in this Bible Study series have an extensive Leader Guide. If you are a participant in a group, a Leader Guide is not necessary, unless you want the author's answers. If you are studying independently, you may want the Leader Guide.

In the Guide the answers follow the questions with a small amount of space for the Leader's personal responses. If you are using the Leader Guide and want to do the study without the influence of the author's answers the best solution is to obtain the blank Worksheets, which are free. This will allow you to record your answers separately before reviewing the answers in the Leader Guide.

See the instructions on the previous "FREE RESOURCES" page to access the free Worksheets.

"Discover the Overlooked.
Apply it to Your Life!"

Book Description

Could One Small Detail in Scripture Transform Your Faith?

Do you ever feel like your faith has become routine, that you're simply going through the motions? Do you yearn for a vibrant connection with Jesus, but struggle to discern His purpose for your life?

"The Chosen Person" invites you on a transformative journey to encounter Jesus in a fresh, powerful way. Through intentional study and Get Wisdom's signature approach to bridging biblical wisdom with everyday application, you'll unlock a deeper understanding of Christ's love and His call on your life. Prepare to step beyond spiritual complacency and embrace a vibrant, purpose-filled faith.

Delve into intimate moments with Melchizedek, a host of angels, Jason, and other misunderstood lives. Gain insights into the true gospel and how it's more than salvation. Find clear and present wisdom that can be applied in a modern era.

Embark on a journey to the soul with this book by Get Wisdom Publishing. Rediscover your enthusiasm for Jesus. Reinvigorate your faith. Be more than you knew you could be.

Unleash the power of Scripture in your life.

Book 9 in the OBSCURE series is all about the person Jesus Christ. We examine a number of characters closely associated with Jesus. The first is the priest Melchizedek. The primary focus of this lesson is on the superiority of Christ and the argument outlined in the book of Hebrews on that subject.

We then examine one of the many scribes identified in the Bible. This is the scribe who said "I will follow you wherever you go," but Jesus questioned his priorities and his commitment.

We examine the lives of Nicodemus and Lazarus as we near the crucifixion. The next lesson is Jesus on the cross with a criminal who knew who Jesus was and said, "Jesus, remember me when you come into your kingdom." Then Jesus made a remarkable promise: "Today you will be with me in Paradise."

Following the crucifixion Jesus appeared to two disciples walking home to Emmaus from Jerusalem. We then find Philip running down a dusty road to talk with an Ethiopian eunuch who had been in Jerusalem.

Lastly, we look at the story in Acts describing Jason who hosted Paul and Silas in Thessalonica. Paul was being pursued and persecuted by the Jews and when they could not find Paul they took their anger out on Jason. This allows us to closely examine the subject of the Messiah.

"Scripture holds answers in unexpected places. Our unique Bible studies reveal overlooked wisdom for today's challenges."

INTRODUCTION

We equip readers with timeless wisdom and practical tools that transform, not just inform. Our books combine deep insights with real-life application to create lasting change.

Description of The OBSCURE Bible Study Series

This unique series uses a number of lesser-known Bible characters and events to explore such major themes as Angels, being Born Again, Courage, Death, Evangelism, Faithfulness, Forgiveness, Grace, Hell, Leadership, Miracles, the Remnant, the Sabbath, Salvation, Rebellion, Sovereignty, Thankfulness, Women, the World, Creation, and End Times.

The series as a whole provides both a broad and fresh understanding of the nature of God as we see Him act in the lives of people we've never examined before.

Most of the people chosen for these studies are unfamiliar because they are mentioned only a few times in Scripture – fifteen only once or twice. Others, although more familiar, are included because of their particular contribution to kingdom work.

For example, Scripture mentions Shamgar only twice. One verse in Judges 3:31 tells his story and 5:6 simply establishes a timeline and says nothing more about him. Then there is Nicodemus, with whom we associate the concept of being "born again." His name appears only 5 times, all in one short passage in the book of John. Eve, although obviously not obscure, is included in order to investigate the creation story.

Group Discussion or Individual Study

These studies can be done individually or in a small discussion group. The real value of the study is in the discussion questions. We all see life differently and the thoughts and ideas shared in a group will often lead to a richer understanding of the Scripture. The questions often require the participant to put himself (herself) in the mind or circumstances of that person in the Scriptures.

The commentary portion of the introductory material in each lesson is there to help clarify the passage and set the stage for the discussion questions. The questions are designed to help the student understand the meaning of the text itself and explore the kingdom implications from a personal point of view.

Ideal For Both New and Mature Bible Students

These lessons have three underlying questions:

- "Who is this person?"
- "What is happening here?"
- "What is the implication for my life?"

Because of the obscurity of the characters under study, chances are that even experienced participants with prior understanding of the lesson's theme will find fresh material to explore. Both new and long-time students will be challenged by the life lessons these unfamiliar characters can teach them.

Format of Lessons

Each lesson begins with the Scripture using the ESV translation followed by short sections titled "Context," "What Do We Know," and "Observations." The discussion questions are designed to help the student understand the subject and are followed by several application questions.

"We believe applied wisdom empowers life change. Our books provide clarity, inspiration, and tools to equip readers to live their best life."

Melchizedek
the priest of Jerusalem

Occurrences of "Melchizedek" in the Bible: 10

Themes: Priesthood; Superiority of Christ

Scripture

Genesis 14:17-20

After his return from the defeat of Chedorlaomer and the kings who were with him, the king of Sodom went out to meet him at the Valley of Shaveh (that is, the King's Valley). 18 And Melchizedek king of Salem brought out bread and wine. (He was priest of God Most High.) 19 And he blessed him and said, "Blessed be Abram by God Most High, Possessor of heaven and earth; 20 and blessed be God Most High, who has delivered your enemies into your hand!" ESV

Ps 110:4   *The Lord has sworn and will not change his mind, "You are a priest forever after the order of Melchizedek."* ESV

Heb 5:4-10   *And no one takes this honor for himself, but only when called by God, just as Aaron was. 5 So also Christ did not exalt himself to be made a high priest, but was appointed by him who said to him, "You are my Son, today I have begotten you"; 6 as he says also in another place, "You are a priest forever, after the order of Melchizedek."*

7 In the days of his flesh, Jesus offered up prayers and supplications, with loud cries and tears, to him who was able to save him from

death, and he was heard because of his reverence. 8 Although he was a son, he learned obedience through what he suffered. 9 And being made perfect, he became the source of eternal salvation to all who obey him, 10 being designated by God a high priest after the order of Melchizedek. ESV

Heb 6:19-20   We have this as a sure and steadfast anchor of the soul, a hope that enters into the inner place behind the curtain, 20 where Jesus has gone as a forerunner on our behalf, having become a high priest forever after the order of Melchizedek. ESV

Heb 7:1-21   For this Melchizedek, king of Salem, priest of the Most High God, met Abraham returning from the slaughter of the kings and blessed him, 2 and to him Abraham apportioned a tenth part of everything. He is first, by translation of his name, king of righteousness, and then he is also king of Salem, that is, king of peace. 3 He is without father or mother or genealogy, having neither beginning of days nor end of life, but resembling the Son of God he continues a priest forever.

4 See how great this man was to whom Abraham the patriarch gave a tenth of the spoils! 5 And those descendants of Levi who receive the priestly office have a commandment in the law to take tithes from the people, that is, from their brothers, though these also are descended from Abraham. 6 But this man who does not have his descent from them received tithes from Abraham and blessed him who had the promises. 7 It is beyond dispute that the inferior is blessed by the superior. 8 In the one case tithes are received by mortal men, but in the other case, by one of whom it is testified that he lives. 9 One might even say that Levi himself, who receives tithes, paid tithes through Abraham, 10 for he was still in the loins of his ancestor when Melchizedek met him.

11 Now if perfection had been attainable through the Levitical priesthood (for under it the people received the law), what further need would there have been for another priest to arise after the order of Melchizedek, rather than one named after the order of Aaron? 12 For when there is a change in the priesthood, there is necessarily a change in the law as well. 13 For the one of whom these things are spoken belonged to another tribe, from which no one has ever served at the altar. 14 For it is evident that our Lord

was descended from Judah, and in connection with that tribe Moses said nothing about priests.

15 This becomes even more evident when another priest arises in the likeness of Melchizedek, 16 who has become a priest, not on the basis of a legal requirement concerning bodily descent, but by the power of an indestructible life. 17 For it is witnessed of him, "You are a priest forever, after the order of Melchizedek." 18 On the one hand, a former commandment is set aside because of its weakness and uselessness 19 (for the law made nothing perfect); but on the other hand, a better hope is introduced, through which we draw near to God. 20 And it was not without an oath. For those who formerly became priests were made such without an oath, ESV

The Context

1. First mention (Gen 14) – Abram met Melchizedek in approximately 2000 BC. The Levitical priesthood was established by Moses in approximately 1500 BC.

2. Second mention (Ps 110) – King David mentioned him in approximately 1000 BC [1000 years later].

3. Last eight mentions occur in Hebrews around 60 AD [2000 years later], where the subject is the superiority of Christ.

Melchizedek is mentioned ten times in the Bible, eight of which occur in the Book of Hebrews. The reason for this is that the author of Hebrews is arguing, or demonstrating, the superiority of Christ to the Jewish reader. In order, he argues that Christ is superior to angels, to Moses, to Abraham, and to the Levitical priests. That is when Melchizedek enters the picture. The author says that Jesus is the great high priest and that He is a priest forever, "in the order of Melchizedek." Thus, Jesus is not part of the Levitical system of priests.

What Do We Know?

Melchizedek is a mysterious figure because we really don't know much about him. We know that he was said to be a priest of the

Most High God and the King of Salem, which would have been Jerusalem. We know that Abram (Abraham) offered him a tenth of the spoils of war, implying that Abram considered Melchizedek to have a higher status than himself. Therefore if one can demonstrate that Jesus is higher or greater than Melchizedek, then Jesus is by default greater than Abraham, thus demonstrating the superiority of Christ.

By giving his tithe to Melchizedek, Abram acknowledged his own lower position. Because all Levitical priests were Abram's descendants, they too would hold a position inferior to Melchizedek. Thus the priesthood of Melchizedek is greater than the Levitical priesthood.

Implications and Observations

Why did the Hebrews need a priest? What was the purpose of the priest? Prior to the creation of the Levitical priesthood at Mt. Sinai when Moses received the Law, the "priestly function" was probably performed by the head of the family, clan, or tribe. Moses' brother Aaron was the first High Priest, and according to God's instructions that function would continue through Aaron's descendants. The High Priest held a great deal of power and influence in the lives of the Jewish people. The priestly functions for the Jews were all part of the line of Aaron and the tribe of Levi. But that changed with the arrival of Jesus, whom the author describes as being in the "order of Melchizedek," not Aaron.

Psalm 110 tells us that the Messiah (Jesus) would not only be a king but also a priest, and a priest in the order of Melchizedek. Thus, the implication is that Jesus' priesthood would have some or all of the characteristics of the priesthood of Melchizedek.

> Ps 110:4 *The Lord has sworn and will not change his mind: "You are a priest forever, in the order of Melchizedek." NIV*

Discussion Questions

A. MELCHIZEDEK

A1. Record and list all the things you know or can find out about Melchizedek.

A2. Melchizedek was a priest of the Most High God (Gen 14:18): What do you think it means that Melchizedek was a priest? Who did he represent as a priest?

A3. What other office did Melchizedek hold that might have allowed him to function as a priest?

A4. What are the implications of Hebrews 7:3?
Without father or mother, without genealogy, without beginning of days or end of life, like the Son of God he remains a priest forever. NIV

A5. What interesting occurrence is reported in Genesis 14:20?
Genesis 14:20   *"And blessed be God Most High, who delivered your enemies into your hand." Then Abram gave him a tenth of everything.* NIV

Q. Since the king would normally receive part of the spoils of war, is this a religious tithe or the spoils of war?

B. PRIESTS

B1. Priests represented the people before _____ and conducted their duties by presenting _____ on behalf of the people and the nation to God.

B2. Based on Leviticus 4:20, why was an offering presented by the priest?
Thus shall he do with the bull. As he did with the bull of the sin offering, so shall he do with this. And the priest shall make atonement for them, and they shall be forgiven. ESV

Q. What does "atonement" mean?

B3. The Levites _____ the priests by caring for the Temple (or tabernacle) and helping prepare the sacrifices which the priests would offer on behalf of the people. In presenting these sacrifices, the priests were acting as _____ between God and man.

Q. What is a "mediator"?

B4. Why was a mediator or priest necessary? What did they do for Israel?

C. AARON AND THE LEVITES

C1. How, when, and where did the Levitical priesthood become established?

C2. What does Heb 5:1 and 5:4 tell us about the High Priests?
Heb 5:1, 4   *For every high priest chosen from among men is appointed to act on behalf of men in relation to God, to offer gifts and sacrifices for sins. . . .4 And no one takes this honor for himself, but only when called by God, just as Aaron was. ESV*

C3. What does Heb 2:17 say was a responsibility of the priest?
Therefore he had to be made like his brothers in every respect, so that he might become a merciful and faithful high priest in the service of God, to make propitiation for the sins of the people. ESV

    Q. What does "make propitiation for sins" mean?

        Propitiation [Pro PISH ih a shun] is the concept or the process by which man is reconciled to God. This occurs through Jesus' death (shed blood) which pays the price for our sin, thus satisfying the requirements of a holy God.

C4. What were the inherent limitations of Jewish Levitical priests?

> The priests were normal men, therefore, they were
> themselves inherently _____.
> Since they were normal men they eventually _____
> and their service ended.
> The priest could only temporarily _____ the problem;
> they could not permanently _____
> people.
> Thus the priest could not provide what was needed most:
>
>> Permanent _____ from sin
>> A _____ heart.
>> A right relationship with _____.

D. JESUS, the High Priest

D1. What does Heb 7:16 say that Jesus' priesthood is based on?
Hebrews 7:16   *who has become a priest, not on the basis of a
legal requirement concerning bodily descent, but by the power of
an indestructible life.* ESV

> Q. Why is that important, how does it relate, and what
> does that mean?

D2. What does 7:19 say is a better way than the former
priesthood?
*(for the law made nothing perfect); but on the other hand, a better
hope is introduced, through which we draw near to God.* ESV

D3. How does the author use Melchizedek to show the eternal nature of Jesus' priesthood?

D4. How would you contrast the longevity of the former Levitical priesthood and that of Jesus' priesthood?

D5. What does Hebrews 7:25 say Jesus is doing and what is the significance?
Consequently, he is able to save to the uttermost those who draw near to God through him, since he always lives to make intercession for them. ESV

D6. So what conclusion can you draw from all the above?

E. APPLICATION

E1. Do you believe or feel that you need a priest? Why? Why not?

    a) to approach Jesus?

    b) to approach God, the Father?

    c) to speak to the Holy Spirit?

E2. Do you believe, like the Levitical priests, you must prepare in advance in any way before you approach God?

Scribe
wants to follow Jesus

Occurrences of "scribes" in the Bible: 87

Themes: Count the Cost; Commitment; Priorities

Scripture

Matt 8:18-22   The Cost of Following Jesus
Now when Jesus saw a great crowd around him, he gave orders to go over to the other side. And a scribe came up and said to him, "Teacher, I will follow you wherever you go." 20 And Jesus said to him, "Foxes have holes, and birds of the air have nests, but the Son of Man has nowhere to lay his head." 21 Another of the disciples said to him, "Lord, let me first go and bury my father." 22 And Jesus said to him, "Follow me, and leave the dead to bury their own dead." ESV

Luke 9:57-60   The Cost of Following Jesus
As they were going along the road, someone said to him, "I will follow you wherever you go." 58 And Jesus said to him, "Foxes have holes, and birds of the air have nests, but the Son of Man has nowhere to lay his head." 59 To another he said, "Follow me." But he said, "Lord, let me first go and bury my father." 60 And Jesus said to him, "Leave the dead to bury their own dead. But as for you, go and proclaim the kingdom of God." ESV

The Context

This passage describes the cost or meaning of following Jesus and provide a good example of two people telling the same story with emphasis on different details. Matthew begins the story by saying a scribe came up to Jesus. Luke on the other hand refers to the person as "someone." The authors are probably reporting the same story, but it's very possible that Jesus said this on more than one occasion and the authors are reporting similar stories that occurred at different times. If it is the same story then each author simply chose to emphasize different parts of the same situation.

What Do We Know?

Matthew says that a scribe told Jesus he was going to follow Him. Scribes were sometimes referred to as lawyers or experts in the law. They advised others about the meaning and implications of scripture, and they also may have had certain responsibilities in copying and editing scripture. In some cases they acted as teachers.

Jesus' response to the scribe may appear to be a bit harsh unless Jesus knew something that is not reported in the text. Alternatively, Jesus may have been looking for an opportunity to raise the question of commitment and this was a good opportunity.

Jesus may also have been responding to the scribe's brash statement that he would follow Him "wherever" He would go. This is the kind of overstatement you and I might make in our excitement to be involved but have absolutely no idea of what we are talking about. Jesus likely knew that this was all just talk from this scribe. No one really had any idea yet what it meant to follow Jesus.

Matthew vs. Luke

Let's compare these two passages and observe where they are the same and where they are different.

	Matthew	Luke
Location:	countryside; near the sea	road
Person:	scribe	someone
Address:	Teacher	---
Scribe said:	"I will follow you wherever you go"	same
Jesus response:	"Foxes have holes . . ."	same
Second person:	Another disciple	Not identified
Second inquiry	"Lord, let me first go . . . "	same
Jesus response:	"Follow me, and leave the dead . . ."	#

> #*"Leave the dead to bury their own dead.*
> *But as for you, go and proclaim the kingdom of God."*

Jesus' response to the second inquiry in Luke was substantially different. Luke does not report him saying "Follow me" and at the end Luke adds Jesus' instruction to "go and proclaim the kingdom of God."

Follow Me

The scribe said he would follow Jesus. Jesus often used the word "follow" to indicate an ongoing relationship. It was not meant to describe the act of physically following Jesus around the countryside.

Jesus' invitation to be a disciple was not about serving, working, or preaching. It was to repent and *follow* Him. The Greek word means "to be in the same way with" [i.e. a disciple]. Jesus was inviting people to come along with Him and "buy into His program." He wanted people He could mold into disciples – people growing in knowledge and relationship with Him.

Therefore, we observe throughout the four gospels that Jesus calls disciples to *follow* Him:

> Matt 4:19   Follow me and I will make you fishers of men.
>
> Matt 16:24   If anyone would come after me [*follow*], he must deny himself, take up his cross, and then follow me. [See also Mt 10:37-38]

> Matt 19:21   If you want to be perfect, sell your possessions and give to the poor. That will bring you treasure in heaven. Then <u>follow</u> me.
>
> John 10:27   My disciples listen to my voice; I know them, and they <u>follow</u> me. [Also see John 12:26.]

Therefore, it is very clear that there is a special meaning to the concept of following. It is not referring to a distant relationship but something that takes priority, requires putting others first, and involves a deep commitment.

These passages indicate there will be work involved and a serious commitment required. John talks more about the relationship aspects using the metaphor of sheep describing followers and the nature of the relationship: they are known by Him, they are secure, and they will be with Him.

Discussion Questions

<u>A. GENERAL</u>

A1. Is there any significance in Matthew reporting that the person saying he would follow Jesus anywhere was a scribe?

A2. Did Jesus approach this first individual and ask him to follow?

A3. Does Jesus' response in Mt 8:20 provide any insight into His personal identity and ministry?

A4. What would the scribe have likely known about the designation or name "Son of Man"?

A5. Do you think the scribe really meant that he would follow Jesus anywhere He would go?

A6. How would you characterize the scribe's statement that he would follow Him anywhere?

A7. What do you think Jesus meant by, *"Foxes have holes, and birds of the air have nests, but the Son of Man has nowhere to lay his head?"*

A8. Would the above have any special meaning to the scribe?

A9. One might conclude that Jesus was warning the scribe that it was not an easy life, but what can we conclude about the meaning when Jesus says, *"Follow me, and leave the dead to bury their own dead"*?

A10. The passage in Luke is followed by a third illustration that does not appear in Matthew's account:

> Luke 9:61-62   *Yet another said, "I will follow you, Lord, but let me first say farewell to those at my home." 62 Jesus said to him, "No one who puts his hand to the plow and looks back is fit for the kingdom of God."* ESV

Given Jesus' response in this illustration, how would you interpret and summarize Jesus' teaching in this passage?

A11. How would you compare or contrast Lk 9:23 to these illustrations about following?
Luke 9:23   *And he said to all, "If anyone would come after me, let him deny himself and take up his cross daily and follow me."* ESV

A12. Do you think that the man's father is dead? Why? Why not?

A13. What tendencies of men might Jesus be thinking about when He says there is "no place to lay his head?"

A14. Why do you think Luke adds the statement in 9:60 to "proclaim the kingdom of God"?

A15. In Luke 9:57-62 what is different about the first story compared to the last two?

> Q. Do these excuses sound familiar to anyone? How easy is it for you to put off what you know you should do because you're lazy, complacent, tired, busy, or scared?

A16. One obvious question for the reader is, "How did the scribe and the questioners respond to Jesus' challenge?" What do you think?

A17. Jesus is speaking about our priorities in choosing to follow Him. Specifically in the last two stories (Lk 9:59-62) who or what is to take a lower priority?

> Q. How do you feel about this?

A18. Does your family (spouse, children, parents) take second priority to Jesus?

> Q. Can you think of any situation in your life when you chose Jesus over family? How did the family respond?

B. APPLICATION

B1. Do you consider yourself a follower? Why? Why not?

B2. When you became a Christian did you "count the cost"?

B3. Do you need to stop now and count the cost?

B4. Are you fully committed or only partially committed to your faith?

B5. If you sense you are not fully committed, what <u>one</u> thing could you do that would make a significant difference?

B6. Have you made a complete break with the past or time before you accepted Christ? In Luke 9:62, Jesus said, *"No one who puts his hand to the plow and looks back is fit for the kingdom of God."* ESV Elijah called Elisha as his coworker or assistant and Elisha responded as Christ wants us to respond to His calling. He slaughtered his oxen and burned his farm equipment – he even held a barbecue for his neighbors (1 Kings 19:20-21).
How would you characterize your commitment compared to Elisha?

B7. Are you too comfortable in your relationship with Christ?

Nicodemus
who came at night

Occurrences of "Nicodemus" in the Bible: 5

Themes: Born Again

Scripture

John 3:1-15   Jesus and Nicodemus

Now there was a man of the Pharisees named Nicodemus, a ruler of the Jews. 2 This man came to Jesus by night and said to him, "Rabbi, we know that you are a teacher come from God, for no one can do these signs that you do unless God is with him." 3 Jesus answered him, "Truly, truly, I say to you, unless one is born again he cannot see the kingdom of God." 4 Nicodemus said to him, "How can a man be born when he is old? Can he enter a second time into his mother's womb and be born?" 5 Jesus answered, "Truly, truly, I say to you, unless one is born of water and the Spirit, he cannot enter the kingdom of God. 6 That which is born of the flesh is flesh, and that which is born of the Spirit is spirit. 7 Do not marvel that I said to you, 'You must be born again.' 8 The wind blows where it wishes, and you hear its sound, but you do not know where it comes from or where it goes. So it is with everyone who is born of the Spirit."

9 Nicodemus said to him, "How can these things be?" 10 Jesus answered him, "Are you the teacher of Israel and yet you do not understand these things? 11 Truly, truly, I say to you, we speak of what we know, and bear witness to what we have seen, but you do not receive our testimony. 12 If I have told you earthly things and you do not believe, how can you believe if I tell you heavenly things? 13 No one has ascended into heaven except he who descended from heaven, the Son of Man. 14 And as Moses lifted up the serpent in the wilderness, so must the Son of Man be lifted up, 15 that whoever believes in him may have eternal life." ESV

John 7:50-52
Nicodemus, who had gone to him before, and who was one of them, said to them, 51 "Does our law judge a man without first giving him a hearing and learning what he does?" 52 They replied, "Are you from Galilee too? Search and see that no prophet arises from Galilee." ESV

John 19:38-41
After these things Joseph of Arimathea, who was a disciple of Jesus, but secretly for fear of the Jews, asked Pilate that he might take away the body of Jesus, and Pilate gave him permission. So he came and took away his body. 39 Nicodemus also, who earlier had come to Jesus by night, came bringing a mixture of myrrh and aloes, about seventy-five pounds in weight. 40 So they took the body of Jesus and bound it in linen cloths with the spices, as is the burial custom of the Jews. ESV

The Context

References to Nicodemus appear only in the book of John, and his meeting with Jesus appears early in the book – chapter 3. It appears in the storyline after Jesus has performed His first miracles by turning water into wine and chasing the money changers out of the Temple.

I suspect John very deliberately placed this visit with Nicodemus in chapter 3 in order to establish early the important concept of being born again. The famous verse John 3:16 is placed immediately following Jesus' explanation of what it means to be born again.

Whereas the concept of being born again focuses on the individual, the text following John 3:14 focuses on Jesus' purpose with further insight into how man should respond to God. The last half of chapter 3 is the story of John the Baptist and in John, chapter 4, we meet the Samaritan woman at the well.

What Do We Know?

Nicodemus, a Pharisee, came to see Jesus at night. There is no clear evidence as to why Nicodemus came at night. We do know that Nicodemus said he had certain beliefs:

> 1) he knew Jesus came from God, and
> 2) the miracles Jesus had performed testified to God's hand being on Jesus.

Jesus responded to Nicodemus by saying he must be born again and Nicodemus had no idea what Jesus was talking about. So Jesus explained what He meant:

> 1) we must be born again to enter the kingdom, and
> 2) we must be born of water and the Spirit.

Nicodemus still did not understand and asked for more information. Jesus responded by saying He was not sure Nicodemus was capable of understanding these spiritual things, and He ended the conversation with Nicodemus by revealing certain things about Himself:

> 1) He identified Himself as the "Son of Man," probably implying He fit the reference in Daniel.
> 2) He implied He would be going back to heaven.
> 3) He said He would be "lifted up," meaning He would die (see John 3:14; 8:28; 12:32-34).
> 4) Everyone who believed in Him would receive eternal life.

John 3:16: *For God loved the world in this way: He gave His One and Only Son, so that everyone who believes in Him will not perish but have eternal life.*

Implications and Observations

Being born again is frequently referred to as "new birth," "regeneration," or being a "new creation." The implication of this experience is that one has encountered God in some way and the result is a transformed life because of the indwelling of the Holy Spirit. For example, evidence of the fruit of the Spirit may become obvious:

> Galatians 5:22-23   *But the fruit of the Spirit is love, joy, peace, patience, kindness, goodness, faithfulness, 23 gentleness, self-control; against such things there is no law.* ESV

Another result one might observe is a deep and abiding commitment to spiritual things like humility, conviction of sin, trust in Christ, and real repentance – a truly changed life. A born-again Christian might be actively seeking God, trusting in God's Word, spending time in prayer or any of the other spiritual disciplines.

Being born again is not something we do or earn but something we receive as a free gift. Paul says, "this grace was given to me" (Eph 3:8) and Paul describes salvation as God's gift (Eph 2:8). It is a change that happens in an instant. It changes heart, mind, and soul such that one is a new creation:

> 2 Corinthians 5:17   *Therefore, if anyone is in Christ, he is a new creation. The old has passed away; behold, the new has come.* ESV

It occurs because of God's grace:

> Ephesians 2:4-5   *But God, being rich in mercy, because of the great love with which he loved us, 5 even when we*

were dead in our trespasses, made us alive together with Christ— by grace you have been saved. ESV

The prophets Jeremiah and Ezekiel prophesied the coming church age as a time when one would receive a new heart and a new spirit. Paul says the old will pass away and the evidence of the change will show in our life through acts of love. Although the change is internal (the heart), it is demonstrated by our outward acts of love. John speaks a great deal about loving our brother:

1 John 3:14   *We know that we have passed out of death into life, because we love the brothers. Whoever does not love abides in death.* ESV

This result is inexpressible and glorious joy:

1 Peter 1:8   *Though you have not seen him, you love him. Though you do not now see him, you believe in him and rejoice with joy that is inexpressible and filled with glory,* ESV

Discussion Questions

A. GENERAL

A1. Why do you think Nicodemus came to visit Jesus? What are the logical reasons that a man like Nicodemus might make this visit?

A2. What can we learn about Nicodemus from:

Jn 3:1 (Pharisee) _____.

Jn 3:1 (ruler) _____.

Jn 19:39 _____.

A3. Why do you think Nicodemus came at night?

A4. How would you describe or explain being "born again?"

A5. What is the theological reason one must be born again?

A6. Why does Nicodemus believe that Jesus came from God (3:2)?

Q. Is this a legitimate reason to believe?

Q. What does John 2:23-25 say about the people who saw the signs and believed?

A7. Based on 3:2 who does Nicodemus believe Jesus to be?

Q. Why would Nicodemus address Jesus as Rabbi?

A8. Nicodemus did not ask about salvation. Why did Jesus reply to Nicodemus about being born again?

A9. In 3:3 what does Jesus say is the result if one is not born again?

Q. What did that mean to the Jewish believer?

A10. In 3:5-6 Jesus repeats what He said in 3:3 but with a bit more information. Again, Jesus says a requirement for entering the Kingdom is being born again. What further clues does Jesus give here about the meaning of being born again?

Born of water: _____.

Born of the Spirit: _____.

Born into the Spirit: <u>I live in the Spirit.</u>

Q. In 3:6 Jesus says, "*Whatever is born of the flesh is flesh, and whatever is born of the Spirit is spirit.*" What does He mean?

A11. How would you relate being born of the Spirit to:
John 1:12-13   *But to all who did receive him, who believed in his name, he gave the right to become children of God, 13 who were born, not of blood nor of the will of the flesh nor of the will of man, but of God.* ESV

A12. In 3:10 what did Jesus do?

Q. Is this a fair accusation?

A13. Could Jesus make this accusation of us today? Do we adequately understand the prophetic scriptures that should concern us today? Can you think of any passages that current believers tend to overlook or put aside as not important that in fact, may be critical to our understanding of:

Salvation: _____.

Christian Life: _____.

The Gospel: _____.

A14. Who is the "Son of Man" (3:13)? How do you know?

A15. What further do we learn from John 8:28, *So Jesus said to them, "When you have lifted up the Son of Man, then you will know that I am he, and that I do nothing on my own authority, but speak just as the Father taught me."* ESV

A16. When everything was said and Nicodemus departed, what do you think he was thinking? What did he actually learn during his visit with Jesus?

A17. Nicodemus may have been embarrassed about coming to Jesus. He never really asked Jesus a question (except in response to Jesus saying he must be born again). We assume that Jesus knew what was on his mind. What's on your mind? If you had one, and only one, question to ask about Christian salvation, what would it be?

A18. The term "born again" only appears in Scripture three times. Is there real meat in this concept or is this all just a story or allegory with limited scope? What descriptive term does Jesus use in all of the following?

3:3 _____.

3:5 _____.

3:11 _____.

B. BORN AGAIN

B1. Based on the following, what do we learn about new birth?

a. _____.
1 Cor 3:1-2   *But I, brothers, could not address you as spiritual people, but as people of the flesh, as infants in Christ. 2 I fed you with milk, not solid food, for you were not ready for it. And even now you are not yet ready*, ESV

b. _____.
Eph 4:22-24   *to put off your old self, which belongs to your former manner of life and is corrupt through deceitful desires, 23 and to be renewed in the spirit of your minds, 24 and to put on the new self, created after the likeness of God in true righteousness and holiness.* ESV

Q. How would you compare this to Ro 12:2?
Rom 12:2   *Do not be conformed to this world, but be transformed by the renewal of your mind, that by testing you may discern what is the will of God, what is good and acceptable and perfect.* ESV

c. _____

1 Peter 1:3   *Blessed be the God and Father of our Lord Jesus Christ! According to his great mercy, he has caused us to be born again to a living hope through the resurrection of Jesus Christ from the dead*, ESV

d. _____

Titus 3:5   *he saved us, not because of works done by us in righteousness, but according to his own mercy, by the washing of regeneration and renewal of the Holy Spirit.* ESV

D. APPLICATION

D1. What is the most important thing you learned from this lesson?

D2. Should anything you learned here change your life in any way?

D3. Do you have a serious or personal question about your spiritual life you need or want to ask somebody?

D4. Are you born again? If you are, what are you doing about it? If you are not, why not?

Lazarus
beggar at Abraham's side

Occurrences of "Lazarus/poor man" in Luke: 4/2

Theme: Hell

Scripture

<u>Luke 16:19-31</u>   The Rich Man and Lazarus Parable
"There was a rich man who was clothed in purple and fine linen and who feasted sumptuously every day. 20 And at his gate was laid a poor man named Lazarus, covered with sores, 21 who desired to be fed with what fell from the rich man's table. Moreover, even the dogs came and licked his sores. 22 The poor man died and was carried by the angels to Abraham's side. The rich man also died and was buried, 23 and in Hades, being in torment, he lifted up his eyes and saw Abraham far off and Lazarus at his side. 24 And he called out, 'Father Abraham, have mercy on me, and send Lazarus to dip the end of his finger in water and cool my tongue, for I am in anguish in this flame.' 25 But Abraham said, 'Child, remember that you in your lifetime received your good things, and Lazarus in like manner bad things; but now he is comforted here, and you are in anguish. 26 And besides all this, between us and you a great chasm has been fixed, in order that those who would pass from here to you may not be able, and none may cross from there to us.' 27 And he said, 'Then I beg you, father, to send him to my father's house — 28 for I have five brothers — so that he may warn them, lest they also come into this place of torment.' 29 But Abraham said, 'They have Moses and the Prophets; let them hear them.' 30 And he said, 'No, father Abraham, but if someone goes to them from the dead,

they will repent.' 31 He said to him, 'If they do not hear Moses and the Prophets, neither will they be convinced if someone should rise from the dead.'" ESV

NOTE: Lazarus is the only character in any of the biblical parables who is mentioned by name.

The Context

Luke includes in chapters 12-18 several teachings and parables by Jesus. There is no particular context to the parable of the rich man and Lazarus. It appears in Luke among a number of other parables with no introduction or explanation. This story does not appear in any of the other Gospels.

The focus of this parable is hell (or Hades). In the Old Testament the name used to represent hell, "Sheol," appears 66 times. The words" hell" and "Hades" each appear 10 times in the New Testament. In Revelation Chapters 19-20 hell is called the "lake of fire" and is used 5 times. Jesus refers to hell as a "blazing furnace" in Matthew when He is telling parables about the Kingdom.

What Do We Know?

Although the terms "hell" and "hades" are most frequently associated with the place where the wicked go, there are a number of other terms or phrases that describe this place:

- the place where the worm does not die,
- the lake of fire,
- the place of unquenchable fire,
- the furnace of fire,
- the blazing fire,
- the place of fire and brimstone
- the black darkness, and
- the eternal fire which has been prepared for the devil and his angels.

These phrases give a terrifying hint to the nature of the place and make it very obvious that one would not want to go there. It is clearly a place of punishment and torment. Even if we believe that these particular description are not to be taken literally, it is obvious that the intent is to describe a place of infinite sadness, regret, and suffering where one is in <u>continual</u> and <u>eternal</u> agony and misery.

Since the story about the rich man in Hades is a parable, we must be careful not to draw too many conclusions from it. It is likely that this parable is not teaching specifically about Hades but is a warning by Jesus to His audience that their refusal to listen, hear, and understand His message could lead to dire consequences.

The parable indicates that Lazarus is at Abraham's side, a place which is "a long way off" from the Rich Man who is in Hades, and there is a great chasm between them that cannot be crossed in either direction. I suspect this part of the parable is true since it is consistent with other teachings about the afterlife. It would be reasonable to conclude the following from this parable:

- death is final – there are no do-overs or second chances,
- there is a difference in the afterlife for the righteous and the unrighteous, and
- there are sufficient warnings in Scripture to alert us to the dangers of sin.

Implications and Observations

Regardless of what you believe about immortality, hell, heaven, or any other afterlife location, it seems obvious that the spirits or souls of men continue on after physical death. Such continuance occurs for both the righteous and the unrighteous.

Luke 16:22 says that the poor man died and was carried away by the angels to Abraham's side. Some translations say "Abraham's bosom," which was a Jewish term for "heaven" or "a place of blessedness" where the Jewish person would go after death. It is also referred to by Paul as "paradise:"

> 2 Corinthians 12:3-4   *And I know that this man was caught up into paradise—whether in the body or out of the body I do not know, God knows— 4 and he heard things that cannot be told, which man may not utter.* ESV

In contrast, the Rich Man went to "Hades," the Greek word for "Sheol" used throughout the Old Testament, describing hell – a place of misery and torment. This would mean that the Rich Man was unrighteous, which is confirmed by the reference to being in agony because of the flame – a likely inference to the "lake of fire."

The general term Hades was usually considered a holding place or temporary place for the dead and there was one place for the righteous and one place for the wicked. It was often considered the place where all the dead went to await assignment to either a good place (like paradise) or a bad place (like hell). The ISBE says that, "The dead were separated into compartments, the righteous staying in an apparently pleasant place and various classes of sinners undergoing punishments in other compartments." The concept of two places in Hades is implied in Proverbs 14:32 "*The wicked is overthrown through his evildoing, but the righteous finds refuge in his death.* ESV

The place for the righteous dead had several names in the New Testament: Abraham's bosom (Luke 16:22), paradise (Luke 23:43), and Hades (Acts 2:27, 31). In the New Testament the righteous dead believers went at once to be with the Lord:

> 2 Cor 5:8   *Yes, we are of good courage, and we would rather be away from the body and at home with the Lord.* ESV (See also Php 1:23)

The different afterlife result for the righteous and the wicked is confirmed by the parable of the Rich Man. Lazarus was by Abraham's side and the Rich Man in a place of torment. Ps 1 clearly draws a distinction between the righteous person and the sinner:

> Psalms 1:4-6   *The wicked are not so, but are like chaff that the wind drives away. 5 Therefore the wicked will not stand in the judgment, nor sinners in the congregation of the righteous; 6 for the Lord knows the way of the righteous, but the way of the wicked will perish.* ESV

Discussion Questions

A. GENERAL

A1. Is anything about hell or Hades inconsistent with your thoughts about God?

A2. How do you feel about discussing hell? Is this a subject you would prefer left alone? Do you have a problem with a loving God making provision for sinners to spend eternity in hell?

A3. Do you think anyone could make a reasonable argument that there is no real hell?

B. The Parable

B1. What is the length of the period of torment for those in hell?

B2. Is there any evidence that the period of suffering in hell can be cut short or terminated by repentance or by annihilation?

B3. Is the sentence for the unrighteous just? Is it too severe? Why? Why not?

B4. Do you know or have you seen any Scripture that indicates that one does not experience pain, torment, or anguish of some kind in hell?

B5. Why do you think that the poor man, Lazarus, is mentioned by name?

B6. Do you think that this parable is about being poor or rich?

Q. If yes, explain.

Q. If no, then why does Jesus use these opposite terms to identify the two men?

B7. Since Lazarus went to Abraham's side and the Rich Man went to Hades, what can we conclude about these two characters and their relationship to God?

Lazarus: _____.

Rich Man: _____.

B8. Based on this Parable, what might we conclude about hell in the following verses from Luke?

16:23: _____.

16:25: _____.

16:26: _____.

16:30: _____.

16:31: _____.

B9. Where is Lazarus located in this story when he is alive?

Q. What does that mean or imply about the Rich Man?

B10. The Rich Man did not remove Lazarus from his gate. There is no evidence that he refused him the bread scraps, and nothing is said about abuse in any way. So what was the rich man's sin that caused him to end up in hell?

B11. Do you think it is right that the Rich Man's request to warn his brothers was refused?

C. HELL

C1. Why does a place like hell have to exist?

C2. How is hell described in Mark 9:42-44 and what does it mean?

Mark 9:42-44   *Whoever causes one of these little ones who believe in me to sin, it would be better for him if a great millstone were hung around his neck and he were thrown into the sea. 43 And if your hand causes you to sin, cut it off. It is better for you to enter life crippled than with two hands to go to hell, to the unquenchable fire.* ESV

Q. What is the moral of the story in this passage?

C3. Why would Luke say that the one to fear is the One who has authority to assign people to hell (Luke 12:5)?
But I will warn you whom to fear: fear him who, after he has killed, has authority to cast into hell. Yes, I tell you, fear him! ESV

Q. Does this literally mean that God throws people into hell?

If yes, explain?_____.

If no, explain? _____.

C4. What do we learn about hell (the lake of fire) in Rev 20:10?
and the devil who had deceived them was thrown into the lake of fire and sulfur where the beast and the false prophet were, and they will be tormented day and night forever and ever. ESV

C5. What do the following proverbs tell us about the "house of the wicked"?

Pr 3:33   _____.

Pr 14:11   _____.

Pr 21:12   _____.

C6. What do we learn about God's Kingdom in Mt 13:47-50 (Parable of the Net)?

Matt 13:47-50   *Again, the kingdom of heaven is like a net that was thrown into the sea and gathered fish of every kind. 48 When it was full, men drew it ashore and sat down and sorted the good into containers but threw away the bad. 49 So it will be at the close of the age. The angels will come out and separate the evil from the righteous 50 and throw them into the fiery furnace. In that place there will be weeping and gnashing of teeth.* ESV

> Q. What does this parable teach about the ultimate separation of good and bad?

> Q. What does the Parable of the Net mean for us today? (This is the same as the Parable of the Weeds in Mt 13:24-30.)

> Q. How should this concept apply to our lives today?

> Q. What does this say about keeping public or flagrant sinners out of the church?

BONUS QUESTION: If at the end of the Millennium, God annihilated all those in Hell, would that violate His character?

D. APPLICATION

D1. Are you personally comfortable with the concept of hell?

   If no, or probably not, what is your concern?

   If yes, why?

D2. Mark 9 suggests it is better to cut off a body part rather than allow it to cause you to go to hell. The meaning here is that hell is a bad place and should be avoided at all costs. Is there anything you need to do to be right with God?

Criminal
on the cross

Occurrences of "Criminals" in the Bible: 6

Themes: Salvation

Scripture

Luke 23:32-43

Two others, who were criminals, were led away to be put to death with him. 33 And when they came to the place that is called The Skull, there they crucified him, and the criminals, one on his right and one on his left. 34 And Jesus said, "Father, forgive them, for they know not what they do." And they cast lots to divide his garments. 35 And the people stood by, watching, but the rulers scoffed at him, saying, "He saved others; let him save himself, if he is the Christ of God, his Chosen One!" 36 The soldiers also mocked him, coming up and offering him sour wine 37 and saying, "If you are the King of the Jews, save yourself!" 38 There was also an inscription over him, "This is the King of the Jews."

39 One of the criminals who were hanged railed at him, saying, "Are you not the Christ? Save yourself and us!" 40 But the other rebuked him, saying, "Do you not fear God, since you are under the same sentence of condemnation? 41 And we indeed justly, for we are receiving the due reward of our deeds; but this man has done nothing wrong." 42 And he said, "Jesus, remember me when you come into your kingdom." 43 And he said to him, "Truly, I say to you, today you will be with me in Paradise." ESV

NOTE: This event is also mentioned in Mark 15:27 and Matthew 27:38-44, but neither provides any additional information than what is contained in the Luke passage.

The Context

Jesus' final path to the Cross began when He was identified by Judas to the Jewish leaders and temple police on the Mount of Olives (Garden of Gethsemane). After that, He was taken to the house of the high priest. He was next examined by the Jewish Sanhedrin. Then the whole assembly of Jewish leaders took Him to Pontius Pilate who found no reason to charge Jesus with the things they accused Him of. When Pilate learned He was a Galilean he sent Him to Herod. Herod questioned Jesus, and mocked Him by dressing Him in a bright robe and then sent Him back to Pilate. Pilate didn't really want to deal with the situation because he did not feel that Jesus deserved to die. So Pilate gave the people a choice of one "criminal" to set free, Jesus or Barabbas. The Jewish leaders and the people chose to release Barabbas, and insisted that Jesus be crucified. Pilate granted their demands.

Crucifixion was a horrible and brutal form of death. The victim could be on the cross for days before the victim died and the authorities took down the body. No one ever came off a cross alive. Crucifixion was reserved for the worst of criminals, and in particular those whose death the Romans wanted to make a public spectacle in order to discourage future occurrences of the same kind of offense. Crosses were often erected along busy thoroughfares so travelers would see the offenders' agony and their rotting bodies.

What Do We Know?

We do not know much about the two criminals on the cross other than they are described as "criminals." These men not only broke the law but they were likely guilty of much more or they would not have faced crucifixion. Since they were originally scheduled to die with Barabbas, who was a revolutionary (John 18:40), they were also probably guilty of some form of rebellion against the Romans.

These were real criminals hanging on either side of Jesus. They were not minor offenders.

Just Punishment

The two criminals were being punished justly (23:41). They deserved to be there. The insulting criminal "railed" at Jesus as well as the officials but the rebuking criminal seemed to know who Jesus was and rebuked the other criminal. The rebuking criminal appeared to know about Jesus' circumstances because he said:

- Don't you even fear God?
- We are punished justly.
- Jesus has done nothing wrong.
- Jesus, remember me when You come into Your Kingdom.

The two criminals had a different view of the Cross. One was defiant, challenging, and insulting. But the rebuking criminal saw the truth, understood his real need, and asked to be remembered by Jesus. We have no way of knowing how or why this one criminal knew the truth about Jesus. Most of us would be like the insulting criminal and be complaining, "I haven't done anything wrong," or "I don't deserve this." The rebuking criminal seemed to understand the justice of the punishment and its implications.

Salvation by Grace

A revealing statement by the rebuking criminal was, "*Jesus, remember me when You come into Your kingdom!*" This statement has to mean that the criminal knew who Jesus was and that he was thinking about the future. Given the situation one must conclude that the criminal probably believed that Jesus was the Messiah or he would not have been talking about the future kingdom. It is remarkable what the rebuking criminal seemed to know and understand.

Obviously Jesus knew his heart and rewarded him with that promise we all hope to hear – *I will see you in Paradise*. Jesus specifically said, "*Truly, I say to you, today you will be with Me in Paradise.*" This is one of the clearest pictures of grace in the New Testament. The criminal received something he obviously did not deserve or earn. This criminal did absolutely nothing except ask in faith to be remembered. His reward was totally undeserved.

Implications and Observations

GRACE
This story is very simple and can tell us a great deal about salvation. It is completely consistent with:

> Ephesians 2:8-9   *For by grace you have been saved through faith. And this is not your own doing; it is the gift of God, 9 not a result of works, so that no one may boast.* ESV

Grace abounds! The criminal did absolutely nothing to warrant salvation. We can only assume that a change of heart had occurred and at some point he came to know Jesus as the Messiah and believe He would return to set up His kingdom. That belief is evidenced by his statement that Jesus would be entering into His kingdom.

WORKS:
Works have nothing to do with salvation. We don't earn salvation in any way. We are made right with God only through the sacrifice Jesus made. There are no scales weighing our good against our bad. If you have even a tiny bit of feeling that some form of works is required to enter the Kingdom, then how do you explain that this criminal is saved? If works of any kind are necessary, how does this man make it?

RITUALS:
Salvation has nothing to do with performing rituals:

- Baptism: The criminal was not and never will be baptized! Baptism is only a public testimony or symbol of an inward change that has occurred. Jesus saw the inward change, but we cannot.

- Communion: The Lord's Supper is not a requirement for salvation – it's a remembrance. Communion is a picture of what Christ did for us and His instruction was to remember Him.
- Catechisms (classes): Obviously the criminal did not have time to get off the cross and take 6 weeks of classes. Completing a course of classes does not make you a believer or give you salvation.
- Church: Church attendance or membership in a particular denomination does not get you saved. No one person, church, or denomination owns the Gospel message. The Gospel produces a personal relationship with Christ. You don't need a relationship with anyone other than Christ. No middleman is necessary for anything. Although pastors, priests, and church leaders can be helpful, they only exist to help, guide, and teach.
- Sinner's Prayer: This criminal said nothing except to ask Jesus to remember him. He didn't walk an aisle or sign a card. Although he asked to be remembered, he did not pray or ask in any way for the things we often think must be said in a sinner's prayer.
- Spiritual Gifts: There was no evidence of the criminal speaking in tongues or using any other spiritual gift.
- Forgiveness: We have no knowledge of the criminal asking for forgiveness for his sins.
- Repentance: Since Jesus accepted Him into the Kingdom we can only assume that Jesus knew that his heart was right, but we have no evidence in the text that the criminal ever repented.

TODAY IN PARADISE

What does the word "Paradise" refer to? Most all commentaries and Biblical dictionaries indicate that this term generally refers to a place like the Garden of Eden, or some beautiful peaceful place. It might even allude to a heaven-like place or a place of future happiness and joy. In my view the actual place is not the critical understanding we should be searching for. Rather, we should recognize it as a good place and the real news is that the criminal will be there with Jesus, *today.*

What do we learn or can we logically conclude about the words of assurance that Jesus provided the criminal? Note that Jesus began the statement by saying, "Truly I say to you." This phrase is used when something very important is about to be said. Jesus is saying, "I really want you to hear what I am about to say, so listen up! This is really important! Don't miss it!"

Jesus says, *today!* It is not tomorrow or after three days, but *today* you will be in Paradise with *Me.* This would certainly confirm the Scripture which says "absent from the body, present with the Lord" (2 Cor 5:8).

The criminal clearly demonstrates that there is no Purgatory that must be visited before he can be with Jesus. It is clearly stated that the criminal would be with Jesus, today, in Paradise.

LIFE LESSONS:

a. As long as I am alive it is not too late to turn to Christ!
b. I just need to believe in Jesus to be saved!
c. I don't have to earn my way to heaven; it's all grace.

Discussion Questions

GENERAL

A1. Do you think the criminal who rebuked the other criminal was given the truth supernaturally or did he come to this understanding about Jesus in some other way? Explain.

A2. How would the criminal know that Jesus "had done nothing wrong"?

A3. When the criminal says, *"Jesus, remember me when You come into Your kingdom"* what does the criminal knows about Jesus?

A4. Why do you think that Jesus did not respond to the insulting criminal?

A5. In 23:34 it says that Jesus forgave "them." Who do you think Jesus is referring to? Is it (a) the persecutors in general, (b) the two criminals, (c) the Romans, (d) the Jewish leaders, or (e) everyone?

A6. What do you think is the <u>most</u> significant thing we learn from this passage? Why?

A7. What do you think happened to the insulting criminal?

A8. Who in this story do you identify with most? Why?

B. DIGGING DEEPER

B1. Do you think that Lk 23:40 means that the criminal knew Jesus was God?

Luke 23:40   *But the other rebuked him, saying, "Do you not fear God, since you are under the same sentence of condemnation?"* ESV

B2. Is the question, "Aren't You the Messiah? Save yourself and us!" asked by the insulting criminal legitimate?

B3. Compare what the rebuking criminal says in 23:41 with the reward described in 23:43. What is ironic about what he is getting in one case compared to the other?

Lk 23:41, 43   *"And we indeed justly, for we are receiving the due reward of our deeds; but this man has done nothing wrong."* . . . *43 And he said to him, "Truly, I say to you, today you will be with me in Paradise."* ESV

B4. Do you think the following verse could be used to support the criminal's salvation? How?
Rev 12:11   *And they have conquered him by the blood of the Lamb and by the word of their testimony, for they loved not their lives even unto death.* ESV

C. SALVATION

C1. If you believe that there must be some degree of works involved in salvation, then how do you explain that the criminal will be in Paradise with Jesus, today?

C2. If you think baptism, church membership, a sinner's prayer, spiritual gifts, or asking for forgiveness are required for salvation, then how did the criminal get saved?

C3. Can you find an example of the sinner's prayer in the New Testament? What must be said?

C4. Can you think of any other salvation requirements that man imposes which are questionable given this example of salvation?

C5. What do you think is the minimum necessary for a person to do or say in order to be saved?

C6. Do you think this criminal knew what he was asking for? Do you think he was looking to be "saved"? What do you think was his motive or purpose for asking to be remembered?

D. APPLICATION

D1. If Jesus were sitting next to you, would you recognize Him?

D2. Is your heart ready to hear the Good News? Is your heart ready to hear any news?

D3. Which type of criminal are you? Do you see and understand what is right next to you or are you blinded and focused on yourself?

D4. What do you hope in when trouble hits you?

Emmaus Disciples
two men on road

Occurrences of "Cleopas" in the Bible: 1
(Cleopas, is named; the other is unnamed)

Themes: Post Resurrection Encounters

Scripture

Luke 24:13-35

That very day two of them were going to a village named Emmaus, about seven miles from Jerusalem, 14 and they were talking with each other about all these things that had happened. 15 While they were talking and discussing together, Jesus himself drew near and went with them. 16 But their eyes were kept from recognizing him. 17 And he said to them, "What is this conversation that you are holding with each other as you walk?" And they stood still, looking sad. 18 Then one of them, named Cleopas, answered him, "Are you the only visitor to Jerusalem who does not know the things that have happened there in these days?" 19 And he said to them, "What things?" And they said to him, "Concerning Jesus of Nazareth, a man who was a prophet mighty in deed and word before God and all the people, 20 and how our chief priests and rulers delivered him up to be condemned to death, and crucified him. 21 But we had hoped that he was the one to redeem Israel. Yes, and besides all this, it is now the third day since these things happened. 22 Moreover, some women of our company amazed us. They were at the tomb early in the morning, 23 and when they did not find his body, they came back saying that they had even seen a vision of angels, who said that he was alive. 24 Some of those who were with us went to the tomb and found it just as the women had said, but him they did not see." 25 And he said to them, "O foolish ones, and slow of heart to believe all that the prophets have spoken! 26 Was it not necessary that the Christ should suffer these things and enter into his glory?" 27 And beginning with Moses and all the Prophets, he interpreted to them in all the Scriptures the things concerning Himself.

28 So they drew near to the village to which they were going. He acted as if he were going farther, 29 but they urged him strongly, saying, "Stay with us, for it is toward evening and the day is now far spent." So he went in to stay with them. 30 When he was at table with them, he took the bread and blessed and broke it and gave it to them. 31 And their eyes were opened, and they recognized him. And he vanished from their sight. 32 They said to each other, "Did not our hearts burn within us while he talked to us on the road, while he opened to us the Scriptures?" 33 And they rose that same hour and returned to Jerusalem. And they found the eleven and those who were with them gathered together, 34 saying, "The Lord has risen indeed, and has appeared to Simon!" 35 Then they told what had happened on the road, and how he was known to them in the breaking of the bread. ESV

The Context

Jesus had been crucified and it was the third day, Sunday, the day He was discovered resurrected. Luke 24:1-12 reports that the women had gone to the tomb, found it empty, and had returned to the Apostles to give them the news. Two disciples, Cleopas and a friend, left Jerusalem and were walking along on the road to Emmaus after hearing this news. They were discussing all that had happened – trying to make sense out of three crazy days. They were joined by Jesus on the road, but the two were supernaturally prevented from recognizing Him.

What Do We Know?

It is likely that Jesus caught up with them from the rear, slowed down, and started asking questions, giving the impression He knew nothing about what had happened in Jerusalem. They told Him that they had hoped Jesus would be the Messiah, indicating they probably were not yet convinced that Jesus was alive.

Jesus' initial response to their story was that they were foolish and very slow to believe all that the Prophets had said would happen. He then proceeded to explain the Scriptures that revealed the truth about the Messiah (Himself). Apparently this was not adequate for the two disciples because the text does not indicate they believed. It was not until they had stopped for the evening and were eating supper that Jesus allowed them to understand. Their eyes were opened when He broke the bread and gave thanks. Then, as soon as they recognized Him, He disappeared. The disciples then said a very interesting thing:

> Luke 24:32   . . . *"Did not our hearts burn within us while he talked to us on the road, while he opened to us the Scriptures?"* ESV

The two disciples got up and immediately went back to Jerusalem. Apparently they told the Apostles everything because the text indicates they said they did not recognize Jesus until He broke the bread.

Implications and Observations

One might wonder why this story is in the Bible or why Jesus bothered to spend time on the road with these two. The only obvious result of this appearance of Jesus is that these two become strong believers in the resurrection and they returned to Jerusalem to confirm the resurrection to the Apostles. On the surface this does not seem like a very productive use of Jesus' time. One might wonder if there could have been something more important or significant that Jesus might have been doing?

The verses following indicate that Jesus appeared to this group of disciples in the upper room, including the two who had just returned. He showed them His hands and feet and ate with them. He then opened their minds so they could understand the Scriptures, and told the group to stay in the city until they had been clothed with power from on high – Pentecost!

It appears likely that for some reason Jesus wanted Cleopas and his friend back in Jerusalem to be part of the upper room group. These two had been on their way to Emmaus but Jesus wanted them back with the other disciples. Why? We don't know. Scripture never mentions either of these two again, but that does not mean they were not doing important kingdom work. In fact, they must have been important or Jesus would not have influenced their return to Jerusalem where He would meet with them again.

Only a few were privileged to see and hear Jesus directly that evening in the upper room. These two disciples who had been on the road to Emmaus only hours earlier became part of a unique group of people who saw Him, spoke with Him, ate with Him, and received instructions directly from Him. They also witnessed the Ascension (Lk 24:50-53)!

What if their unbelief had prevented them from recognizing Jesus? How would you feel, looking back, if you had missed out on something like this?

Discussion Questions

GENERAL

A1. Why were these two disciples going to Emmaus? In fact, why were they going anywhere? Why were they leaving the other disciples in Jerusalem?

A2. The text says they were discussing and arguing about the events that had taken place. What might they have been arguing about?

Q. Why did Jesus have to die?

A3. Complete the statements about the key events that are reported as happening in this passage (24:13-35).

a. Two men walked west from Jerusalem to_____.

b. They were discussing the events in Jerusalem:

- chief priests/rulers had handed Jesus over to be _____;
- women found the tomb _____;
- the angels told them Jesus was_____;
- the disciples _____ the women's report.

c. Jesus joined them on the road, walked and talked with them, but they _____ Him.

d. Jesus opened up the Scriptures and _____.

e. Jesus would have gone on, except the men invited Him _____.

f. They _____ together.

g. Their eyes were _____ and they _____
Jesus.

h. Then Jesus _____.

i. The disciples got up and returned to _____.

A3. What is your view or understanding of 24:16...."*but they were kept from recognizing him?*"

A4. In 24:19 they referred to Jesus as a "prophet." Why? What does that tell you about what these two believed?

A5. In 24:21 notice that the disciples mentioned the "third day." It is possible that they were referring to the belief of the Jews that the soul left the body after the third day. But it is more likely they were remembering what Jesus said about "being raised" on the third day (there are 12 such references in the New Testament). This thought may have been one of the things the two were arguing about on the road. What do you believe they were thinking about in this context?

NOTE: Luke 9:22   *"The Son of Man must suffer many things and be rejected by the elders and chief priests and scribes, and be killed, and on the third day be raised."* ESV

A6. In 24:30 Luke reports that Jesus took the bread, broke it, and gave thanks. Why? Who should have given the blessing?

A7. What was inherently happening when Jesus prayed and gave thanks? How might this have contributed to the disciples recognizing him?

A8. What other reason associated with the breaking of the bread might have contributed to the disciples recognizing Jesus?

A9. Why were the two returning to Jerusalem?

A10. Luke 24:32 reports that the disciples' hearts burned within them when Jesus talked with them on the road. Why do you suppose they said nothing at that point? Would you have revealed the feeling if you had been one of the two men?

Q. Has anything like this ever happened to you?

A11. In none of the other post-resurrection appearances of Jesus are the disciples prevented from recognizing Him. Why do you think Jesus did that in the case of these two disciples?

A12. Is the unnamed disciple a man or woman? Could you make an argument for the companion of Cleopas being a woman?

B. DIGGING DEEPER

B1. What theological or spiritual concepts are confirmed by the passage above (Luke 24:13-35)?

a. The _____ actually happened.

b. The tomb was _____.

c. God is sovereign. He has the divine prerogative to keep us blinded to His presence if that suits Him.

d. Jesus associated Himself with the _____ (24:26).

e. Jesus had to _____ and then be _____ (24:26).

f. The church can be _____ to believe the Bible. (24:25).

g. God Himself will cause us to _____.

B2. What did Jesus mean in 24:26 when He said that He will enter into His glory?

B3. How does Hebrews 1:3 support what you found in B2?
Hebrews 1:3   *He is the radiance of the glory of God and the exact imprint of his nature, and he upholds the universe by the word of his power. After making purification for sins, he sat down at the right hand of the Majesty on high.* ESV

Q. What characteristic does John 2:11 reveal about Jesus?

John 2:11   *This, the first of his signs, Jesus did at Cana in Galilee, and manifested his glory. And his disciples believed in him. ESV*

B4. In 24:27 Jesus is said to have explained the Scriptures relative to Himself. If that explanation included the following passages, what would Jesus have revealed to the two disciples?

Isa 7:14 _____.
Isa 7:14   *Therefore the Lord himself will give you a sign. Behold, the virgin shall conceive and bear a son, and shall call his name Immanuel. ESV*

Micah 5:2_____.
Micah 5:2   *But you, O Bethlehem Ephrathah, who are too little to be among the clans of Judah, from you shall come forth for me one who is to be ruler in Israel, whose origin is from of old, from ancient days. ESV*

Mal 3:1 _____.
Mal 3:1   *Behold, I send my messenger and he will prepare the way before me. And the Lord whom you seek will suddenly come to his temple; and the messenger of the covenant in whom you delight, behold, he is coming, says the Lord of hosts. ESV*

Zech 13:7_____.
Zechariah 13:7   *"Awake, O sword, against my shepherd, against the man who stands next to me," declares the Lord of hosts. "Strike the shepherd, and the sheep will be scattered; I will turn my hand against the little ones. ESV*

Zech 12:10_____.
Zechariah 12:10   *"And I will pour out on the house of David and the inhabitants of Jerusalem a spirit of grace and pleas for mercy, so that, when they look on me, on him whom they have pierced, they shall mourn for him, as one mourns for an only child, and weep bitterly over him, as one weeps over a firstborn." ESV*

Jer 31:31-32_____.
Jeremiah 31:31-32   *"Behold, the days are coming, declares the Lord, when I will make a new covenant with the house of Israel and the house of Judah, 32 not like*

the covenant that I made with their fathers on the day when I took them by the hand to bring them out of the land of Egypt, my covenant that they broke, though I was their husband, declares the Lord." ESV

Hosea 2:23_____.
Hos 2:23   "*and I will sow her for myself in the land. And I will have mercy on No Mercy, and I will say to Not My People, 'You are my people'; and he shall say, 'You are my God.'" ESV*
Rom 9:24-25   *even us whom he has called, not from the Jews only but also from the Gentiles? 25 As indeed he says in Hosea, "Those who were not my people I will call 'my people,' and her who was not beloved I will call 'beloved.'" ESV*

B4. What did the two disciples tell the group in Jerusalem when they returned (24:35)?

Q. What might they have wanted to keep hidden?

B5. These two disciples were in the upper room when Jesus appeared to the group of disciples gathered there (24:42-49). What important information did they observe and hear directly from Jesus because they were in that group?

a. They observed Jesus _____ boiled fish like any other person who was alive.

b. He said that everything that was _____ about Him in the Old Testament would be fulfilled.

c. Their minds were opened to _____ the Scriptures – the same thing He did for the two disciples on road to Emmaus.

d. Jesus told them to stay in Jerusalem until they received _____ (Pentecost).

C. APPLICATION

C1. Have you ever been surprised by Jesus' presence? Where? How? Why?

C2. Has Jesus ever been walking along with you and you did not recognize Him?

C3. What keeps you from recognizing Him or knowing that He may be near?

C4. Are you actually looking for Him? In Scripture? In worship? In your work? In your quiet times?

C5. Upon recognizing Jesus, the disciples rushed back to tell their friends. Do you have a friend who needs to hear about your encounter with Jesus?

Ethiopian Eunuch
Philip baptized

Occurrences of "Ethiopian Eunuch" in the Bible: 5

Themes: Evangelism; Gospel; Opportunities

Scripture

Acts 8:26-40

Now an angel of the Lord said to Philip, "Rise and go toward the south to the road that goes down from Jerusalem to Gaza." This is a desert place. 27 And he rose and went. And there was an Ethiopian, a eunuch, a court official of Candace, queen of the Ethiopians, who was in charge of all her treasure. He had come to Jerusalem to worship 28 and was returning, seated in his chariot, and he was reading the prophet Isaiah. 29 And the Spirit said to Philip, "Go over and join this chariot." 30 So Philip ran to him and heard him reading Isaiah the prophet and asked, "Do you understand what you are reading?" 31 And he said, "How can I, unless someone guides me?" And he invited Philip to come up and sit with him. 32 Now the passage of the Scripture that he was reading was this:

"Like a sheep he was led to the slaughter
and like a lamb before its shearer is silent,
so he opens not his mouth.
33 In his humiliation justice was denied him.
Who can describe his generation?
For his life is taken away from the earth."

34 And the eunuch said to Philip, "About whom, I ask you, does the prophet say this, about himself or about someone else?" 35 Then Philip opened his mouth, and beginning with this Scripture he told him the good news about Jesus. 36 And as they were going along the road they came to some water, and the eunuch said, "See, here is water! What prevents me from being baptized?" 38 And he commanded the chariot to stop, and they both went down into the water, Philip and the eunuch, and he baptized him. 39 And when they came up out of the water, the Spirit of the Lord carried Philip away, and the eunuch saw him no more, and went on his way rejoicing. 40 But Philip found himself at Azotus, and as he passed through he preached the gospel to all the towns until he came to Caesarea. ESV

The Context

We first met Philip when he was chosen along with Stephen as one of the seven godly men to serve the Greek widows who had been overlooked in the food distribution (Acts 6:5). When persecution broke out against the Christians following Stephen's stoning, Philip went to Samaria:

> Acts 8:5-6   *Philip went down to the city of Samaria and proclaimed to them the Christ. 6 And the crowds with one accord paid attention to what was being said by Philip when they heard him and saw the signs that he did.* ESV

The road from Jerusalem to desert Gaza (50-60 miles) was well-traveled. On the road Philip was instructed to approach a chariot carrying an Ethiopian official. He was a eunuch, an official in charge of the treasury for Candace, queen of Ethiopia. Obviously he was an important and influential person in the Ethiopian government. A eunuch originally referred to a castrated male who was often in charge of royal harems. However, over time the term came to refer simply to trusted officials, with or without any kind of deformity.

The eunuch would have been either a proselyte or a God-fearer in the Jewish faith:

> PROSELYTE: A true follower who took on the Law for themselves, including circumcision.

> GOD-FEARER: A follower who attended the synagogue and read Jewish scriptures, but was not circumcised.

The eunuch was probably a Gentile God-fearer who believed in the One True God, read the Scriptures, but was not circumcised or necessarily committed to following the Law.

What Do We Know?

God wanted the eunuch to hear the Gospel, so much so that He sent an angel to direct Philip to the caravan carrying the government official back home to Ethiopia. The official was ready to hear the Gospel when Philip arrived: he was reading about the suffering servant in Isaiah.

It does not say how many people were traveling with the eunuch, but given his high standing he certainly would not have been traveling alone. There is a high probability that it was a sizable group. One can imagine the scene with Philip running along the road to catch up with the chariot and then jumping on board.

The text says that the eunuch had gone to Jerusalem to worship, but as a eunuch his access to the temple and temple grounds would have been limited. This indicates that the man was very serious about his faith or he would not have made such a long journey. The fact that he was reading Isaiah shows his commitment and desire to seek spiritual knowledge and understanding. This commitment is affirmed again when he immediately asked Philip to explain the Scriptures. The Spirit of God seemed to be at work in the eunuch's heart drawing him to the point of response to the Gospel. He just needed to hear it!

> Romans 10:14-15   *But how are they to call on him in whom they have not believed? And how are they to believe in him of whom they have never heard? And how are they to hear without someone preaching? 15 And how are they to preach unless they are sent? As it is written, "How beautiful are the feet of those who preach the good news!"* ESV

Implications and Observations

Seize the Opportunity: the Gospel

Philip followed the instructions of the angel and immediately went to the Gaza road. He neither questioned nor delayed, but just went. We should all be as quick to obey the instructions and nudges of God! Philip was obedient and the eunuch was open for help. When God leads it is time to follow.

The eunuch was reading the Scriptures and Philip used that situation as a springboard to talk about Jesus. Philip asked the eunuch if he could help. That is a question we could all use to open spiritual conversations: "How can I help?" This spiritual conversation was ready to proceed since the eunuch was reading from Isaiah. Philip knew enough Scripture to recognize what the eunuch was reading and he used the opportunity to propel the conversation to the Gospel message.

Seize the Opportunity: Baptism

Given that the eunuch was likely traveling with an entourage and that the road was well-traveled, it is possible that there was a small crowd witnessing the baptism. The text does not describe the body of water but it was big enough for them to go into and perform the baptism. The text describes an immersion baptism, as they, "went down into" and "came out of" the water. How often do you find a body of water in the desert? Seize the opportunity!

<u>God Knew</u>

It seems clear that God wanted the eunuch to hear the Gospel so he would take it back to Ethiopia. God knew the God-fearing eunuch was ready to accept the message of Christ. God knew that the eunuch was reading Isaiah. God sent the angel to Philip to tell him to approach the chariot. God knew that the eunuch was ready to take the Gospel home with him. God knew it all! God wants to help accomplish the commission He gave His people to take the Gospel to the ends of the earth.

Discussion Questions

A. EUNUCH

A1. What do we actually know about the physical condition of the eunuch?

A2. If the eunuch was emasculated and not allowed beyond the Court of the Gentiles, why would he come to Jerusalem all the way from Ethiopia? [Dt 23:1 *No one whose testicles are crushed or whose male organ is cut off shall enter the assembly of the Lord. ESV*]

A3. Why would the Christian Gospel be attractive to an emasculated eunuch?

A4. Does this mean that in Judaism the eunuch was treated unfairly?

A5. Do you know any group today that might feel unwanted or not welcome like the emasculated eunuch?

Q. Why do you think this division, separation (segregation) occurs?

A6. Fill in the blanks describing what we know about the eunuch and what he did.

The eunuch was an Ethiopian official in charge of the _____.

He worked for _____ (the Queen of Ethiopia).

He was in Jerusalem to _____ the LORD.

He was returning home, riding in a _____ on the Gaza road.

He was reading from the book of _____.

He was probably a <u>"God-fearer."</u>

He was open to <u>listening and understanding</u>.

       Q. Why a eunuch? If the text simply described this person as a "high official" would any meaning be lost because he was not identified as a eunuch?

A7. The text says that the eunuch "went on his way rejoicing." What do you think that means?

<u>B. GENERAL</u>

B1. Who is "the angel of the Lord" in 8:26, "the Spirit" in 8:29, and "the Spirit of the Lord" in 8:39?

B2. How did Philip respond to the angel?

B3. What can you find out about *"the road that goes down from Jerusalem to desert Gaza?"*

B4. Does this road sound like a very exciting place to be sent? Why? Why not?

      YES: _____.

      NO: _____.

B5. How would you have reacted if some dirty, dusty character ran up to your chariot and asked, "Do you understand what you're reading?"

But this government official said, "Sure, I'm always open to someone else's opinions. Jump in."

Q. How did the eunuch get a copy of Isaiah? What form would this be printed on?

Q. Do you think that Philip just ran up to the chariot and started this conversation?

B6. List the providential things God is doing in this story.

Q. Describe the major obstacles that Philip could have or might have encountered in approaching the official.

B7. What lessons do we learn from Philip's actions?

a. He was _____ to the Spirit.

b. He recognized what the eunuch was reading, so he _____ Scripture.

c. He asked a _____ question.

d. He was capable of using _____ to describe Jesus, the Messiah, and the Gospel.

B8. Why do you suppose the eunuch couldn't understand what he was reading?

C. DIGGING DEEPER

C1. How would you walk somebody through the Bible telling them about Jesus? What key Scriptures would you use to lead an individual to Christ?

C2. What key principle of evangelism do you observe here?

C3. Isaiah's Servant Songs include:

The passage in Isaiah that the eunuch was reading was from Song #4. In these "songs" the Savior (Messiah) is pictured and characterized as a servant. He is also related to or contrasted with Israel and is described as being the perfect Israel. But the servant is mostly described in more human terms. For example, He will be crushed and suffer (53:10), but be resurrected (53:11), and He will win the victory, bearing the sins of many.

Isaiah 53:7-8 *He was oppressed and afflicted, yet He did not open is mouth. Like a lamb led to the slaughter and like a sheep silent before her shearers, He did not open His mouth. 8 He was taken away because of oppression and judgment; and who considered His fate? For He was cut off from the land of the living; He was struck because of My people's rebellion.*

Q. The eunuch seemed to be having trouble understanding the identity of the one unjustly "led like a sheep to the slaughter." His question relates to the identity of the servant. What are the possible answers to his question?

C4. How does Jesus fit the description in the Fourth Servant Song?

Isaiah 53:5 *But He was _____ because of our _____, crushed because of our _____; punishment for our peace was on Him, and we are healed by His _____.*
Isaiah 53:11 *He will see it out of His anguish, and He will be satisfied with His knowledge. My righteous servant will _____ many, and He will carry their iniquities.*

C5. Why would this be considered an excellent place to start an explanation of the Gospel?

D. BAPTISM

D1. The eunuch asked, "What would keep me from being baptized?" If you were to answer that question, what would you say? What are the minimum requirements for someone to be saved?

Q. How long do you think Philip was talking with the eunuch?

D2. The eunuch said, "*I believe that Jesus Christ is the Son of God.*" Do you think that is enough to baptize the eunuch?

D3. Why do you think the eunuch wanted so badly to be baptized?

D4. What principles do we learn about baptism from this passage?

Q. How would you explain to someone the need to be baptized and the freedom not to be baptized?

E. APPLICATION

E1. Who has been your Philip?

E2. Have you been a Philip recently? Do you need to be? Do you need to ask someone if you can help them?

E3. How much trouble do you have understanding Bible passages? Do you need a Philip?

E4. Do you know any person today who might feel like the eunuch? Is God calling you to talk with them?

Jason
the host

Occurrences of "Jason" in the Bible: 4

Themes: Hospitality; Messiah; Persecution

Scripture

Acts 17:1-10

Now when they had passed through Amphipolis and Apollonia, they came to Thessalonica, where there was a synagogue of the Jews. 2 And Paul went in, as was his custom, and on three Sabbath days he reasoned with them from the Scriptures, 3 explaining and proving that it was necessary for the Christ to suffer and to rise from the dead, and saying, "This Jesus, whom I proclaim to you, is the Christ." 4 And some of them were persuaded and joined Paul and Silas, as did a great many of the devout Greeks and not a few of the leading women. 5 But the Jews were jealous, and taking some wicked men of the rabble, they formed a mob, set the city in an uproar, and attacked the house of Jason, seeking to bring them out to the crowd. 6 And when they could not find them, they dragged Jason and some of the brothers before the city authorities, shouting, "These men who have turned the world upside down have come here also, 7 and Jason has received them, and they are all acting against the decrees of Caesar, saying that there is another king, Jesus." 8 And the people and the city authorities were disturbed when they heard these things. 9 And when they had taken money as security from Jason and the rest, they let them go. 10 The brothers immediately sent Paul and Silas away by night to Berea, and when they arrived they went into the Jewish synagogue.
ESV

The Context

While in Philippi on their second missionary journey, Paul and Silas had been beaten and imprisoned until a midnight earthquake opened all the prison cell doors. Instead of escaping, they had remained in their cells, which led the jailer to ask, "What must I do to be saved?" He and his whole family were saved and baptized. In the morning, the magistrates told Paul and Silas that they were released. But Paul, claiming his Roman citizenship, protested that they had been beaten and imprisoned without a trial and demanded to be escorted from the prison. They were escorted out and told to leave the city, which they did after first meeting with the brothers. They then traveled about 100 miles to Thessalonica, where there was a Jewish community.

Although Paul became known as the Apostle to the Gentiles, he always went first to the local synagogue to speak when arriving in a new town. In Philippi, the text says he "reasoned" with them on three Sabbaths, speaking about Jesus.

What Do We Know?

Paul and Silas spent several weeks explaining that Jesus was the Messiah and had to die and be raised from the dead. The result of that preaching and teaching was that some were persuaded:

> 1) a great number of God-fearing Greeks, and
> 2) a number of leading women in the city.

But that created a problem. Those who did not believe became jealous and gathered a group of troublemakers together, formed a mob, and started a riot. The text says they attacked Jason's house – apparently the place where Paul was staying. They wanted to bring Paula and Silas out into some kind of public assembly where they could inflict serious harm and maybe even death.

We can reasonably assume that Jason was a believer and that he had welcomed into his home Paul and Silas and perhaps others traveling with them as well. But the crowd could not find them. So they grabbed Jason as the next best thing and brought him before the city authorities. The crowd claimed Jason was at fault because:

> 1) Paul and Silas were "turning the world upside down."
> 2) Jason received them as guests.
> 3) They were all acting contrary to Caesar's decrees, claiming that Jesus was king.

The Jews continued to stir up the crowd. Probably in an effort to appease and disperse the crowd, the city officials required Jason and the others from his household to post a security bond, after which they were released. The nature or amount of the security bond is not revealed.

Implications and Observations

Paul spent time trying to convince the Jewish men in Thessalonica that Jesus was the Messiah. He would likely have pointed out Messianic prophecies that Jesus fulfilled. Micah 5:2 says that the one whose origin is from antiquity, from eternity, would be born in Bethlehem. When King Herod, at Jesus' trial, asked where the Christ was to be born, the Jewish leaders confirmed that it was in Bethlehem of Judea. (Mt 2:1-6) There are other prophecies that most Christians today have read or heard about:

- The Messiah would come from the tribe of Judah (Gen 49:10),
- He would be of the house of David (Isa 11:1; Jer 33:21),
- He would be born of a virgin (Isa 7:14),
- He would die by crucifixion (Ps 22:1-21), and
- He would rise again from the dead (Ps 16:8-11).

Jesus fulfills, or will fulfill, every Biblical prophecy about the Messiah. In the following table, match the Old Testament prophecies with their corresponding fulfillments in the New Testament.

EXERCISE:

In the space following the letter in the left column write the number of the fulfilling passage from the right column. How many can you match correctly?

Prophecies about the Messiah

New Testament Fulfillment

A __*5__ Isaiah 40:3, 5   3 A voice of one crying out: Prepare the way of the Lord in the wilderness; make a straight highway for our God in the desert. . . 5 And the glory of the Lord will appear, and all humanity will see it together . .
*A messenger will announce His coming.

1   Matthew 3:16-17   . . . The heavens suddenly opened for Him, and He saw the Spirit of God descending like a dove and coming down on Him. 17 And there came a voice from heaven: This is My beloved Son. I take delight in Him!

B__*9__ Psalms 69:8   I have become a stranger to my brothers and a foreigner to my mother's sons
*He will be shunned by His own brothers.

2   Luke 22:48   48 but Jesus said to him, "Judas, are you betraying the Son of Man with a kiss?"

C__*1__ Psalms 2:7   I will declare the Lord's decree: He said to Me, "You are My Son; today I have become Your Father."
*He is the Son of God.

3   Luke 1:33   He will reign over the house of Jacob forever, and His kingdom will have no end.

D__*7__ Isaiah 6:9-10   And He replied: "Go! Say to these people: Keep listening, but do not understand; keep looking, but do not perceive. 10 Dull the minds of these people; deafen their ears and blind their eyes; otherwise they might see with their eyes and hear with their ears, understand with their minds, turn back, and be healed."   *He would teach in parables.

4   Matthew 27:46   At about three in the afternoon Jesus cried out with a loud voice, "Elí, Elí, lemá sabachtháni?" that is, "My God, My God, why have You forsaken Me?"

E__*2__ Psalms 41:9   Even my friend in whom I trusted, one who ate my bread, has lifted up his heel against me.
*He would be betrayed.

5   Luke 3:4-6   3 He went into all the vicinity of the Jordan, preaching a baptism of repentance for the forgiveness of sins, 4 as it is written in the book of the words of the prophet Isaiah: A voice of one crying out in the wilderness: "Prepare the way . . ."

F__*10__ Isaiah 53:12   12 Therefore I will give Him the many as a portion, and He will receive the mighty as spoil, because He submitted Himself to death, and was counted among the rebels; yet He bore the sin of many and interceded for the rebels.
*He would be put to death with criminals.

6   Mt 22:44   The Lord declared to my Lord, "Sit at My right hand until I put Your enemies under Your feet."

G__*4__ Psalms 22:1   22 My God, my God, why have You forsaken me? Why are You so far from my deliverance and from my words of groaning?
*He would be forsaken by the Father.

7   Matthew 13:34-35   34 Jesus told the crowds all these things in parables, and He would not speak anything to them without a parable, 35 so that what was spoken through the prophet might be fulfilled: I will open My mouth in parables . . .

H__*8__ Psalms 16:10   For You will not abandon me to Sheol; You will not allow Your Faithful One to see the Pit.
*He would be resurrected.

8   Matthew 28:5-6   5 But the angel told the women, "Don't be afraid, because I know you are looking for Jesus who was crucified. 6 He is not here! For He has been resurrected, just as He said. . . ."

I__*6__ Psalms 110:1   The Lord declared to my Lord: "Sit at My right hand until I make Your enemies Your footstool."
*He would be seated at the right hand of God.

9   John 1:11   He came to His own, and His own people did not receive Him.

J__*3__ Daniel 2:44   In the days of those kings, the God of heaven will set up a kingdom that will never be destroyed, and this kingdom will not be left to another people. It will crush all these kingdoms and bring them to an end, but will itself endure forever.
*He will be anointed and eternal.

10   Matthew 27:38   Then two criminals were crucified with Him, one on the right and one on the left.

There are other prophecies that may have been meaningful at that time, since only a few years had passed since Jesus' actual death and resurrection:

- The Messiah would be falsely accused.
- He would be hated without cause.
- His hands and feet would be pierced.

- He would be mocked and ridiculed.
- Soldiers would divide His garments.
- He would pray for His enemies, and
- He would ascend to heaven.

Discussion Questions

GENERAL

A1. Why would Paul want to go to Thessalonica?

A2. Why does 17:2 say "as was his custom" Paul went to the synagogue?

Q. What is a synagogue?

A3. Who were the God-fearing Greeks? What makes them "God-fearing"?

PROSELYTE vs. GOD-FEARING

"Proselyte" is used in a specific sense to designate Gentile converts who had committed themselves to the teachings of the Jewish faith or who were attracted to the teachings of Judaism. A full-fledged proselyte, or convert to Judaism, underwent circumcision and worshiped in the Jewish temple or synagogue. They also observed all rituals and regulations concerning the Sabbath, clean and unclean foods, and all other matters of Jewish custom.

Tired of pagan gods and heathen immorality, these Gentiles came to the synagogues to learn of the one true God and of His call to holiness, justice, and mercy. Many of them accepted the religion, morality, and life-style of the Jews. Not all Gentile sympathizers went so far as to be circumcised, but by New Testament times proselytes were nevertheless a significant part of Judaism, as the references to them in the Book of Acts (2:10; 6:5; 13:43) make clear. These "halfway proselytes" proved to be a rich mission field for the early church. Unable to accept the binding requirements of the Jewish law, many of them turned to Christianity. This new faith in Jesus welcomed all people, regardless of their background, culture, or religious tradition.[1]

A4. When the text says Paul "reasoned" with them from the Scriptures, what does that mean? What were the subjects he would have "reasoned" about?

A5. Acts 17:5 says the Jews became jealous. What would they be jealous of?
Acts 13:45   *But when the Jews saw the crowds, they were filled with jealousy and began to oppose what Paul was saying by insulting him.*

A6. How do you think Jason would feel about his house being attacked? Would he be glad they could not find Paul or upset about all the problems his guests brought on him and his household?

A7. In the Jewish culture what would have been Jason's responsibility as a host?

A8. They charged Jason with "receiving them as guests" (17:7). What was the crime?

A9. The crowd accused them of "turning the world upside down." What was the basis for this charge?

Q. The Jews were upset with Paul's religious teaching, but when Jason and his friends were dragged into court, what were they charged with?

Q. How would the Jesus-followers have felt about what they were doing and what was happening?

A10. How did Jason respond to all the accusations?

A11. What did it mean and what are the implications of Jason having to post bond?

A12. Where does 17:10 indicate Paul went when he left at night?

Q. The brothers sent Paul and Silas off to Berea as soon as it was dark (at night). Why at night? Were they afraid?

A13. This is about the sixth time Paul is forced to leave an area where he is preaching and teaching. Based on 1 Thess 2:1-6, what did Paul say about his visit?

For you yourselves know, brothers, that our coming to you was not in vain. 2 But though we had already suffered and been shamefully treated at Philippi, as you know, we had boldness in our God to declare to you the gospel of God in the midst of much conflict. 3 For our appeal does not spring from error or impurity or any attempt to deceive, 4 but just as we have been approved by God to be entrusted with the gospel, so we speak, not to please man, but to please God who tests our hearts. 5 For we never came with words of flattery, as you know, nor with a pretext for greed— God is witness. 6 Nor did we seek glory from people, whether from you or from others, though we could have made demands as apostles of Christ. ESV

B. DIGGING DEEPER

B1. Acts 17:3 says that Paul explained why Jesus had to die and be raised from the dead. What would Paul have argued and why?

B2. Did Jesus ever say or imply He was the Messiah? Can you find one or more examples in Scripture?

B3. In addition to accusing them of hosting Paul and Silas, they made a more serious charge concerning Caesar. What did they say and what did they mean?

Q. Whether Jesus or Caesar was to be LORD was the real underlying issue for these Christians. Have you ever been in a similar conflict with your faith, where other "authorities" were claiming or demanding your loyalty but it conflicted with your Christian faith?

B4. How does this charge about being a "king" contrast with the charge against Jesus in Luke 23:2?
And they began to accuse him, saying, "We found this man misleading our nation and forbidding us to give tribute to Caesar, and saying that he himself is Christ, a king." ESV

Q. Do you think the local authorities had any grounds for being concerned about Jesus being King?

B5. How would you contrast *blaspheme* relative to being a Jew and *treason* relative to being a Roman citizen?

C. APPLICATION

C1. Have you ever gotten into serious trouble for something you did not do?

C2. What risks are you willing to assume for your faith?

C3. Have your ever "reasoned" with anyone about the scriptures? Could you?

C4. Have you ever been afraid because you are a believer? If so, what did you learn? What would it be like to be in a foreign country where Christianity is hated?

C5. Have you ever publically stood up for your faith like Jason who posted a bond?

Transformation Road Map
Primary Takeaways

1: Jesus is described as a high priest "in the order of Melchizedek," which signifies His superiority over the Levitical priesthood and establishes Him as an eternal and universal high priest, fulfilling biblical prophecies and demonstrating His divine authority.

2: Following Jesus requires a deep and serious commitment, involving more than physical accompaniment, but a profound relationship and prioritization of His teachings above all else.

3: Being "born again" is a transformative spiritual experience, given by God's grace, that results in a new creation with a changed heart, mind, and soul, evidenced by the fruit of the Spirit and a deep commitment to Christ.

4: The parable of the rich man and Lazarus illustrates a stark contrast in the afterlife between the righteous and the unrighteous, emphasizing the finality of death and the importance of heeding spiritual warnings in this life.

5: Salvation is achieved solely through God's grace, evidenced by the criminal on the cross who, despite his lack of works, rituals, or outward displays of faith, was promised paradise simply by acknowledging Jesus and asking to be remembered.

6: After the resurrection, Jesus prioritized reconnecting with and strengthening the faith of his followers, as demonstrated by his journey to Emmaus where he revealed himself and reignited their belief.

7: God's desire to spread the Gospel is demonstrated by Philip's divinely guided encounter with the Ethiopian eunuch, indicating the Importance of obedience, seizing opportunities, and knowing God will orchestrate events to bring individuals to faith.

Free PDF
MAKE WISE DECISIONS
[Get the ebook version for 99 cents]

Consequences Shape Lives.

This book discusses the nature of decisions and explores eight essential questions to make better decisions.

You are a few decisions away from transforming your life. You can make better decisions! This resource has sections on what makes a poor decision, questions to ask yourself, traps to avoid, short and sweet decisions, the wise decision framework, and twenty ways to be wise. It also has a handy decision-making checklist. (12 pages)

Free PDF: https://getwisdompublishing.com/resource-registration/

Kindle ebook for 99 cents: https://www.amazon.com/dp/B0FG8NC53J

Ebook

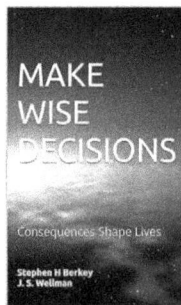
MAKE WISE DECISIONS
Consequences Shape Lives
Stephen H Berkey
J. S. Wellman

Free PDF

Ten Steps to Wise Choices

Timeless Wisdom. Practical Tools. Lasting Impact.

Free PDF
Life Improvement Principles
[Get the ebook version for 99 cents]

You can live your best life!

Welcome to a journey of discovery! In case you have forgotten, your actions have consequences. Unlock your potential! This book (60+ pages) provides the overview of all our strategies and wisdom principles to live your best life. You *can* transform your life! Get your wisdom-based roadmap to a better life and unlock all the possibilities for growth and success.

Free PDF: https://getwisdompublishing.com/resource-registration/

Kindle ebook for 99 cents:
https://www.amazon.com/dp/B0FG883K7M

Ebook

Life Improvement Principles

You can live your best life!

Stephen H Berkey
J. S. Wellman

Free PDF

Make it your life goal to be the best you can be!

Discover Wisdom and live the life you deserve.

Next Steps!

Continue Studying the *OBSCURE* Series
The *OBSCURE* Bible Study Series
https://www.amazon.com/dp/B08T7TL1B1

Be Challenged by the Jesus Follower Series
The Jesus Follower Bible Study Series
https://www.amazon.com/dp/B0DHP39P5J

Tackle Wisdom-Driven Life Change
Apply Biblical Wisdom to Live Your Best Life!
"Effective Life Change"
https://www.amazon.com/dp/1952359732

Know What You Should Pray
Personal Daily Prayer Guide
https://www.amazon.com/What-Should-Pray-Personal-Journal/dp/1952359260/

Decide to be the Very Best You Can Be
The Life Planning Series
https://www.amazon.com/dp/B09TH9SYC4

You Can Help:

SOCIAL MEDIA: Mention The *OBSCURE* Bible Study Series on your social platforms. Include the hashtag #obscurebiblestudy so we are aware of your post.

FRIENDS: Recommend *OBSCURE* to your family, friends, small group, Sunday School class leaders, or your church.

REVIEW: Please give us your honest review at
https://www.amazon.com/dp/1952359244

The *OBSCURE* Bible Study Series

Continue your journey through the hidden wisdom of Scripture with the OBSCURE Series.

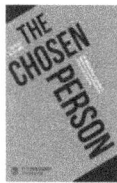

Blasphemy, Grace, Quarrels & Reconciliation: The lives of first-century disciples.
This book presents Joseph of Arimathea, Joanna, Ananias, Hymenaeus, and Cornelius (a centurion). It illustrates the nature and challenges of life as a first-century disciple.

The Beginning and the End: From creation to eternity.
This book has four lessons from Genesis and four from Revelation covering creation, rebellion, grace, worship, and eternity. God is leading us to worship in the Throne Room.

God at the Center: He is sovereign and I am not.
This book examines the virgin birth, worship, prayer, the sovereignty of God, compromise, and trust. God is at the center of all these stories. He is at the center of our lives.

Women of Courage: God did some serious business with these women.
This book examines the lives of Jael, Rizpah, the woman of Tekoa, Tabitha, Shiphrah, and Lydia. These women exhibit great courage and faithfulness. God used them in amazing ways.

The Beginning of Wisdom: Your personal character counts.
In this book we find courage, loyalty, thankfulness, love, forgiveness, and humility. Personal character counts. Decisions have consequences. Wisdom will help us stand firm in our faith.

Miracles & Rebellion: The good, the bad, and the indifferent.
God hates sin and loves to heal the faithful. The rebellion of Korah, Haman, and Alexander compare to the healing stories of Aeneas, a slave girl, and the crippled man at Lystra.

The Chosen People: There is a remnant.
This book concentrates mostly on Israel in the Old Testament, but also covers some interesting subjects as Lucifer, Michael the archangel, and Job's wife.

The Chosen Person: Keep your eyes on Jesus.
The focus is on Jesus and the superiority of Christ. We investigate Melchizedek, the disciples on the road to Emmaus, Nicodemus, and the criminal on the cross.

WEBSITE: http://getwisdompublishing.com/products/
AMAZON: www.amazon.com/author/stephenhberkey

Jesus Follower Bible Study Series

The Jesus Follower Bible Study Series will provide you with a complete description of the nature, characteristics, obligations, commitments, and responsibilities of a true Jesus follower.

Go to our Amazon Book Series page for your copy:
https://www.amazon.com/dp/B0DHP39P5J

The RELATIONSHIP CHARACTERISTICS of a Jesus Follower:
> Are you right with God?

The ONE ANOTHER INSTRUCTIONS to a Jesus Follower:
> Are you right with one another?

The WORSHIP of a Jesus Follower:
> Is your worship acceptable or in vain?

The PRAYER of a Jesus Follower:
> What Scripture says about unleashing the power of God.

The DANGERS of SIN for a Jesus Follower:
> God HATES sin! He abhors sin!

The FOCUS for a Jesus Follower:
> Keep your eyes fixed on Jesus!

The HEART Requirements of a Jesus Follower:
> Follow with all your heart, mind, body, and soul!

The COMMITMENTS of a Jesus Follower:
> Practical Christian living and discipleship.

The OBEDIENCE Requirements for a Jesus Follower:
> Ignore at your own risk!

"Get Wisdom Publishing creates wisdom-driven products that equip readers with timeless insights, understanding, and actionable tools to transform their lives."

Life Planning Series

Read these books if you want to live a better life.

The primary audience for this series is the secular self-help market, but the concepts are Christian based.

CHOOSE FAITH	**For the spiritual seeker and those with spiritual questions.** *Your Spiritual Guidebook For Questions About Religion, God, Heaven, Truth, Evil, and the Afterlife.* https://www.amazon.com/dp/1952359473
CHOOSE CORE VALUES	**Core values will drive your life.** https://www.amazon.com/dp/195235949X

Other Titles in the Life Planning Series
CHOOSE Integrity
CHOOSE Friends Wisely
CHOOSE The Right Words
CHOOSE Good Work Habits
CHOOSE Financial Responsibility
CHOOSE A Positive Self-Image
CHOOSE Leadership
CHOOSE Love and Family
LIFE PLANNING HANDBOOK A Life Plan Is The Key To Personal Growth https://www.amazon.com/gp/product/1952359325

Go to:

https://www.amazon.com/dp/B09TH9SYC4

to get these books.

Personal Daily Prayer Guide
Prayer Resource and Journal

This is a great resource to kick-start your prayer life!

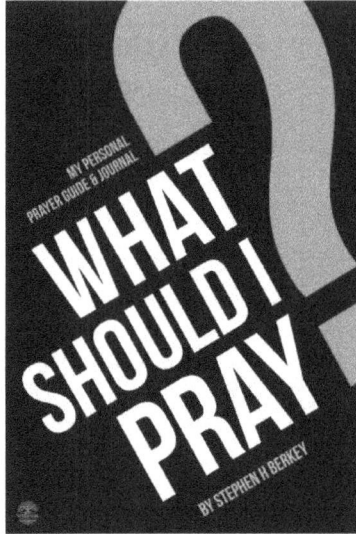

Know what to pray.
Pray based on Bible verses.
Strengthen your prayer life.
Access reference resources.
Pray with eternal implications.
Write your own prayers if desired.
Organize and focus your prayer time.
Learn what the Bible says about prayer.
Find encouragement and advice on how to pray.
Reduce frustration and distraction in your prayer time.

Get your copy today!

https://www.amazon.com/What-Should-Pray-Personal-Journal/dp/1952359260/

Acknowledgments

Arlene
Arlene has served as wife, editor, and proof-reader for all of my writing – thank you for your patience, help, and love.

Michelle
Michelle, our older daughter, has been an invaluable resource. She has graciously produced the website at www.getwisdompublishing.com. She was the first author in the family: graceandthegravelroad.com.

Stephanie
Our middle daughter designed all the covers for the *OBSCURE* Bible Study Series, as well as the marks and logos for Get Wisdom Publishing. We are grateful for her talent!

KOINONIA Small Group
These dear friends have hung in there with me as I taught many of the lessons to them first. Their input, answers, and suggestions have been invaluable.

God, Jesus, and Holy Spirit
Thank you, Lord, for Your guidance and direction.

Notes

1 Nelson's Illustrated Bible Dictionary, Copyright © 1986, Thomas Nelson Publishers; from PC Study Bible, "Scribe."

2 Nelson's Illustrated Bible Dictionary, Copyright © 1986, Thomas Nelson Publishers; from PC Study Bible, "Son of Man."

3 Nelson's Illustrated Bible Dictionary, Copyright © 1986, Thomas Nelson Publishers; from PC Study Bible, "Born Again."

4 Nelson's Illustrated Bible Dictionary, Copyright © 1986, Thomas Nelson Publishers; from PC Study Bible, "New Birth."

5 Easton's Bible Dictionary, PC Study Bible formatted electronic database Copyright © 2003, 2006 Biblesoft, Inc. "Son of Man." All rights reserved.

6 Nelson's Illustrated Bible Dictionary, Copyright © 1986, Thomas Nelson Publishers; from PC Study Bible, "Synagogue."

7 Nelson's Illustrated Bible Dictionary, Copyright © 1986, Thomas Nelson Publishers; from PC Study Bible, "Proselyte."

About the Author

Steve attended church as a child and accepted Christ when he was 10 years old. But his walk with Jesus left a lot to be desired for the next 44 years. In 1994 he "wrestled" with God for some period of months and in September of that year totally surrendered his life to Jesus.

In 1996 he was so driven to study God's Word that he attended the Indianapolis campus of Trinity Evangelical Divinity School (Chicago) to earn a Certificate of Biblical Studies. His hunger for God's Word led him to lead and write all his own Bible studies for his small group. He has been an entrepreneur and Bible study leader for the past 30 years.

He is a member of The Church at Station Hill in Spring Hill, TN, a regional campus of Brentwood Baptist (Brentwood TN).

GETWISDOM
PUBLISHING

www.getwisdompublishing.com

"Get Wisdom Publishing is dedicated to being the trusted source of wisdom-driven books that inspire growth, guide decisions, and empower readers to live with purpose and fulfillment."

Contact Us

Website: www.getwisdompublishing.com

Email: info@getwisdompublishing.com

Facebook: Get Wisdom Publishing

Author's Page: www.amazon.com/author/stephenhberkey

Amazon's Obscure Bible Study Series page:
https://www.amazon.com/dp/B08T7TL1B1

"Go beyond devotionals.
Experience biblical wisdom in action!"

www.ingramcontent.com/pod-product-compliance
Lightning Source LLC
Chambersburg PA
CBHW070812050426

42452CB00011B/2011